Office for National Statistics
Social Survey Division

Smoking, drinking and drug use among young teenagers in 1998

Volume 1: England

Eileen Goddard
Vanessa Higgins

London: The Stationery Office

© Crown copyright 1999
First published 1999
ISBN 011 621263 2

Designed by Adkins Design
Cover: Library photographs

Contents

Acknowledgements

Social surveys are always the work of a team. The authors take full responsibility for the content of this report, but gratefully acknowledge the contribution of those colleagues who carried out the fieldwork and assisted with the editing and other stages of the survey.

The authors thank schools for their co-operation and, most important of all, the pupils who took part in the survey.

Notes to tables

1. A few children failed to answer each question. These 'no answers' have been excluded from the analysis, and so tables that describe the same population may have slightly varying bases.

2. Probabilities of selection varied according to school year (see Chapter 1) and data have been reweighted to adjust for this. Since the reweighted data are rounded, totals are not always the sum of the subgroups shown.

   In tables where age or school year is a variable, the base shown for each age group is the number interviewed, rather than the reweighted figure (which would show more 11-13 year olds, for example, and fewer 14 and 15 year olds than actually took part in the survey). In these tables, the bases for individual years of age do not necessarily sum to the total shown, which is the reweighted figure.

3. Percentages based on fewer than 50 cases are shown in brackets because of the relatively large sampling errors attached to small numbers.

4. The following convention has been used

   > 0 = nil or less than 0.5%
   > .. = not applicable

5. In tables where age is a variable, those aged 16 have been included with the 15 year olds. This is because the survey did not include pupils in year 12, and the small number of 16 year olds sampled from year 11 are not representative of all schoolchildren aged 16.

6. The school year classification is based on the years or forms of maintained secondary schools. The school years of pupils attending middle and upper schools and some non-maintained schools have been adjusted accordingly.

Summary of main findings

The main purpose of this latest survey in a biennial series in England was to continue to monitor smoking and drinking among secondary school children aged 11-15, and for the first time to obtain estimates of the prevalence of drug use among this age group.

Prevalence of smoking (Chapter 3)

In 1998, the overall proportion of 11-15 year olds who were regular smokers (smoking at least once cigarette a week, on average) was 11%, compared with 13% in 1996. Continuing the pattern first established in the mid-1980s, prevalence was significantly higher among girls (12%) than among boys (9%).

Although the fall in prevalence between 1996 and 1998 is statistically significant, it may just represent a short term fluctuation, rather than the start of a downward trend.

The proportion of pupils smoking rises with age and progress through the school. Very few pupils are smokers when they start secondary school: among children aged 11 in 1998, only 1% were regular smokers, and four in five had never even tried smoking. By the age of 15, however, 24% of pupils were regular smokers, and only 30% had never tried a cigarette.

Although girls are more likely than boys to be regular smokers, among those who do smoke, boys smoke more cigarettes. In 1998, boys who were regular smokers had smoked an average of 65 cigarettes in the previous week, compared with 49 for girls. Among occasional smokers, too, boys' consumption was higher than that of girls.

The majority of regular smokers, 71%, had recorded more than 20 cigarettes in the diary: indeed almost one third had recorded more than seventy a week, (an average of at least ten cigarettes a day).

Dependence on smoking (Chapter 4)

More than half of all regular smokers said that they would find it difficult to go without smoking for a week, and almost three quarters said that they would find it difficult to give up smoking altogether. Those who had been smoking regularly for more than a year were much more likely to feel dependent than were those who had started smoking more recently.

Only 11% of current smokers said that their family did not mind them smoking, but 44% thought that their families did not know they smoked. Seventeen per cent of current smokers were allowed to smoke at home.

Purchase of cigarettes (Chapter 5)

In 1998, the proportion of children trying to buy cigarettes from a shop fell to 22%, the lowest level in the series of surveys. Furthermore, the proportion of boys and girls who were refused at least once in the last year when attempting to buy cigarettes from a shop rose to its highest level, 43%, in 1998.

However, 78% of smokers who usually bought cigarettes from a shop said that, on the whole, they found it easy to do so. Boys were more likely than girls to say that they found it difficult (26% compared with 18%).

In 1998 as in previous years most smokers bought their cigarettes from shops, with newsagents or tobacconists (65%) and garage shops (35%) being the most common type of retail outlets used. Sixty-one per cent of current smokers were given cigarettes by their friends while over a quarter (28%) bought them from friends and relatives: almost a quarter (24%) said that they bought cigarettes from a machine.

Drinking in the last week (Chapter 7)

Prior to 1998, there was a fairly marked increase in the frequency with which those who drank did so: the proportion of pupils aged 11-15 who had had an drink in the previous week rose from 20% in 1988 to 27% in 1996. In 1998, however, there was a statistically significant fall to 21%. It is not possible to tell whether this is the start of a new trend, or whether, with hindsight, the results for 1998 will seem a little out of line.

The average weekly amount drunk per pupil aged 11-15 in 1998 was 1.6 units (somewhat less than a pint of beer, or its equivalent). This was less than the estimate of 1.8 units in 1996, but still double the figure of 0.8 units in 1990. These average amounts conceal wide variation in the amounts children of this age drink. The overwhelming majority had drunk little or nothing in the previous seven days, and most of the remainder had drunk only modest amounts. However, at the other end of the scale, 4% of boys and 2% of girls had drunk 15 or more units in the previous week.

The fall in average weekly consumption in 1998 is due almost entirely to the fall in the proportion of pupils who had had a drink in the previous week: the average amount drunk last week by those who did drink continued to increase, in 1998, to 9.9 units from 8.4 units in 1996. Thus, although the proportion drinking in the previous week had fallen in 1998 compared with 1996, those who did drink, drank more.

In 1998, 14% of all 11-15 year olds had drunk beer, lager or cider in the last week; 10% had drunk wine, and the same proportion had drunk spirits. Only 7% had drunk alcopops – a marked fall from 14% in 1996.

Usual drinking behaviour (Chapter 8)
The place of drinking mentioned by the highest proportion of drinkers was their own home or the home of a relative or friend - 58% said this was where they usually drank, compared with 23% saying they drank at parties, 12% saying they usually drank in pubs, and 10% in clubs or discos. In addition, 21% of drinkers said they usually drank at places other than those mentioned: this answer would probably have been given mainly by those who drink out in the open - for example in the street or in the park.

Seven in ten of the youngest drinkers said they were usually with their parents when they had an alcoholic drink. At the other end of the age range, although as many as three in ten 15 year olds still drank with their parents, many more said they were usually with friends when they had a drink.

It is against the law for anyone under 18 to buy alcohol in a pub, off-licence, shop or other outlet, but almost half of those who drink (28% of all children aged 11-15) said they did buy alcohol.

By far the most common place of purchase was the off-licence, mentioned by 20% of drinkers. The next most frequently mentioned, by about 10% of drinkers in each case, were a shop or supermarket, a pub or bar, and from a friend or relative. As in 1996, the 1998 data suggest that pupils are able to buy alcohol at an earlier age in shops and off-licences than in pubs and clubs.

Drug use (Chapter 10)
About one third, 34%, of pupils had been offered at least one of a list of illegal drugs. The likelihood of being offered drugs increased with age: 15% of 11 year olds had been offered drugs, compared with 61% of 15 year olds. Boys were more likely to have been offered them than were girls (36% compared with 32%).

Pupils were much more likely to have been offered cannabis (26%) than any other type of drug. Even so, 14% of pupils had been offered stimulants, 8% psychedelic drugs, and glue (also 8%). Four per cent of pupils said they had been offered heroin.

Although 34% of pupils had been offered drugs, a much smaller proportion, 13%, had ever used drugs. The prevalence of drug use increased sharply with age: one third (33%) of 15 year olds had used drugs compared with only 1% of 11 year olds. Again, boys were more likely to have

used drugs than were girls (14% compared with 12%).

Over half (52%) of those who had ever taken drugs had only ever used cannabis, 40% had used cannabis and other drugs, and 9% had used other drugs only.

Of the 13% of pupils who had ever used drugs, about half - 7% of all pupils - had done so in the last month, and a further 4% of pupils had done so in the last year, though not in the last month. Two percent of pupils had last used drugs more than a year ago.

Smoking and drinking (Chapter 12)
Pupils who smoke are more likely to drink than other pupils, and vice versa. This is not simply due to the fact that the prevalence of both behaviours increases with age. Among 15 year olds, for example, 60% of regular smokers, but only 18% of those who had never smoked, said they usually drank at least once a week. Similarly, the proportion of pupils aged 15 who were regular smokers ranged from 7% of those who did not drink, to 38% of those who usually drank every week.

Drug use in relation to smoking and drinking (Chapter 12)
The likelihood of having ever used drugs is strongly related to smoking experience: 63% of regular smokers had used drugs, compared with only 1% of those who had never smoked. Drug use was also related to usual drinking frequency, but a little less strongly than in relation to smoking - 44% of those who drank at least once a week had used drugs, compared with only 1% of those who had never had a drink.

When the different combinations of smoking and drinking behaviour are considered, the association is even more striking. Virtually no children who had never smoked or drunk alcohol had ever used drugs, but as many as 75% of regular smokers who drank at least once a week had done so.

Health education at school (Chapter 13)
In 1998, a higher percentage of pupils remembered receiving lessons on smoking and on healthy eating than on any other topics. The proportion of pupils who remembered receiving health education on smoking has almost doubled since 1986, having risen from 42% then to 78% in 1998. Although fewer pupils remembered health education lessons covering drugs and alcohol than on smoking, the proportion recalling having had such lessons has also almost doubled since the late 1980s: in 1998, 71% of pupils remembered having had a lesson on drugs in the last year, and 66%, one on alcohol.

The association between health education and behaviour (Chapter 13)

If, as some suggest, warning children about the risks of, for example, drug taking, encourages experimentation rather than the reverse, then this survey might expect to find a higher prevalence of smoking among those who remembered having health education lessons about it, and similar associations for drinking and drug use with having had health education on those topics.

Having taken account of age differences, there is no evidence from this survey to suggest that health education encourages the behaviours it is seeking to advise against. However, there is also none showing that, on the whole, those who remember receiving health education on particular topics are taking the advice given.

Comparison of England and Scotland (Chapter 14)

The comparison of results for England with those for Scotland should be treated with caution: since the education system is different in the two countries, the populations covered by the surveys are not of quite the same ages. The net result is that, on average, the sample in Scotland is about six weeks older than the sample in England.

Smoking

Through out the series of surveys, the prevalence of smoking has consistently been higher in Scotland than in England, although in recent years the difference has narrowed and has not been great enough to be statistically significant. In 1998, 11% of 11-15 year olds in England, and 12% of 12-15 year olds in Scotland were regular smokers (smoking at least one cigarette a week).

Pupils in Scotland were more likely than those in England to have tried to buy cigarettes sometime during the last year (30% compared with 22%).

Drinking

As in previous surveys, the proportion of pupils who drank alcohol during the week before the survey was lower in Scotland than in England, and in 1998, 21% of pupils in England, and 19% of those in Scotland, had done so. Average consumption per pupil was also slightly lower in Scotland than in England (1.4, compared with 1.6 units), but the average amount drunk by those who did drink was similar in the two countries. In both England and Scotland, boys were more likely than girls to have drunk alcohol in the previous week, and to have drunk more than girls.

Compared with those in England, pupils in Scotland were less likely to drink at home, at parties, or in a pub or bar, and much more likely to say they usually drank somewhere else – probably indicating that they drank out of doors.

Those in Scotland were also comparatively more likely to drink with friends, and less likely to drink with their parents: 44% of English drinkers said they usually drank with their parents, compared with only 31% of Scottish drinkers.

A sizeable proportion of drinkers in both countries – 53% in England and 47% in Scotland – said that they never bought alcohol. Among those who did buy alcohol, off-licences were the most common place of purchase in both countries.

Drug use

Pupils in Scotland were more likely than those in England to have been offered drugs – in Scotland, 41% had been offered at least one of the drugs on the list they were shown, compared with 34% in England.

They were also more likely to have tried drugs: 18% of pupils in Scotland had used drugs, but only 13% of pupils in England had done so. This overall difference is reflected in the proportions who had used particular drugs: 16% of pupils in Scotland had used cannabis, compared with 12% of pupils in England, and pupils in Scotland were twice as likely to have used psychedelic drugs and glue (in both cases, 4% of pupils in Scotland had done so, compared with 2% of pupils in England).

The differences between the two countries in relation to drug use are too great to be explained by the slight older average age of the sample in Scotland.

1 Introduction

1.1 Background to the survey

This was the latest in a biennial series of surveys of secondary school children and was carried out in England and Scotland at the request of the Department of Health and the Scottish Office Department of Health (now the Scottish Executive Health Department). The results of the survey in Scotland are presented in a separate report.[1]

When the series of surveys began, in 1982, their sole purpose was to provide estimates of the proportion of children aged 11-15 who smoked, and to describe the smoking behaviour of those who did smoke. During the 1980s they monitored changes in the prevalence of smoking among this age group. By 1988, however, it was felt that some questions on smoking could be dropped, and in that year, a short section of questions on drinking was included for the first time. In 1990, the section was expanded to provide estimates of alcohol consumption.

In 1996, the Health Education Authority commissioned the then OPCS to carry out a series of three annual surveys of young people's attitudes towards smoking and their responsiveness to campaigns aimed at discouraging them from smoking. The opportunity was taken of rationalising where possible the topics included on the 1996 DH and HEA surveys, so that the DH one focussed primarily on aspects of smoking behaviour, and the HEA one on attitudes. This allowed additional questions on usual drinking behaviour to be included in the 1996 DH survey.

In the 1998 DH survey, the coverage of smoking was reduced still further: the questions about the smoking behaviour of family members were dropped from the 1998 DH survey but included instead on the HEA one. This was to accommodate the inclusion for the first time of a number of questions about drug use.

In 1998, as in previous surveys, saliva specimens were collected from half the sample of pupils. They were analysed for the presence of cotinine, which is a metabolite of nicotine, to give an indication of exposure to tobacco smoke. The main purpose of this was to enable some validation to be made of the self-reported smoking data.

1.2 Sample coverage

Estimates of the prevalence of smoking were required for the population of secondary school pupils in school years 7 to 11 inclusive; that is, mainly pupils who were aged 11 to 15 at the start of the school year in September 1998.

The survey covered pupils attending all types of Local Education Authority, Grant Maintained, and independent secondary schools, including middle schools with pupils aged 11 and over, but excluding special schools.

To provide better estimates of smoking, drinking, and drug use among the target age group, the sample size was increased in 1998 by oversampling older pupils, among whom prevalence of smoking, drinking and drug use are relatively high: those in school years 10 and 11 were oversampled by a factor of 2.

1.3 Design of the survey

A two-stage sample design was used. At the first stage a sample of schools was drawn, and at the second stage a sample of pupils was selected within each school. A list of secondary schools was extracted from the 1996 school database supplied by the Schools Register for the Department for Education and Employment. The list of schools was stratified by type of school, whether single sex or mixed, and region.

A sample of 200 schools was selected with probability proportional to the number of pupils aged 11-15. This type of sample design enabled roughly equal numbers of pupils to be selected for interview from each school. Further details of the sample are given in Appendix A.

Saliva specimens were collected from all pupils in half the sample of schools. Because of the effect of clustering in the sample design, it is not ideal to have all the pupils in one school allocated to either the saliva or non-saliva sample, but this is more practicable than collecting specimens from half the selected pupils in each school.

All the schools selected were approached (with the permission of their education authorities in the case of LEA maintained schools) and asked if they would be willing to take part in the survey. Each of the co-operating schools was then visited by an ONS interviewer who selected a systematic sample of pupils taken from all the school registers for years 7 to 11 inclusive.

Each school was given copies of a letter from ONS to be sent to parents of the selected children, telling them about the survey, and asking them to reply only if they wished their child not to take part.

The sampled pupils were brought together in a classroom under the supervision of an interviewer but with no teacher present. They were each asked to complete two documents :

1 a questionnaire about smoking, drinking and drug use;

2 a diary in which they were asked to record all cigarettes smoked during the previous seven days.

In those schools where saliva specimens were to be obtained, pupils were asked to put a small dental roll in their mouth, between the cheek and the lower gum, and keep it there for about twenty minutes while they completed the questionnaire. Pupils were made fully aware of the purpose of the procedure and were told that both smokers and non-smokers would have nicotine in their saliva.

Care was taken to protect the confidentiality of pupils' answers and to make them aware that their answers would not be identified with them personally, nor with the school. Questionnaires, diaries, and saliva specimens were linked by means of a serial number only; names were not used on any of the documents.

If four or more pupils were absent at the main visit, the interviewer made a follow-up visit to the school several days later, if possible checking beforehand that pupils who were absent at the main visit were back in school.

1.4 **Response**

Information was obtained from 4752 pupils in the 147 co-operating schools, 85% of those selected for interview. Taking into account non-response among eligible schools as well as among pupils in co-operating schools, the overall response rate was 62%.

The overall response rate was much lower than in previous years. Response rates among pupils were down a little, from 87% in 1996 to 85% in 1998, but the main factor contributing to the overall fall in response was the poor response rate (74%) among schools, in spite of strenuous efforts to persuade them to take part. Before the start of the survey there was concern that the inclusion of questions on drug use might deter some schools from taking part, but in the event there was no evidence to support this. The most common reasons given by head teachers for not allowing their school to take part in the survey related to pressure of work - inspections, the national curriculum, and other burdens on school administration.

One factor which may have influenced schools in deciding whether or not to take part was the request to take saliva specimens in half the schools. This was never the reason offered for not wishing to take part, but whereas 78% of the control sample of schools took part, only 69% of those in the saliva sample did. In all but one out of the five earlier surveys since saliva testing was introduced in 1988, it appeared to have no effect on response, so it may be that the difference this time is a coincidence.

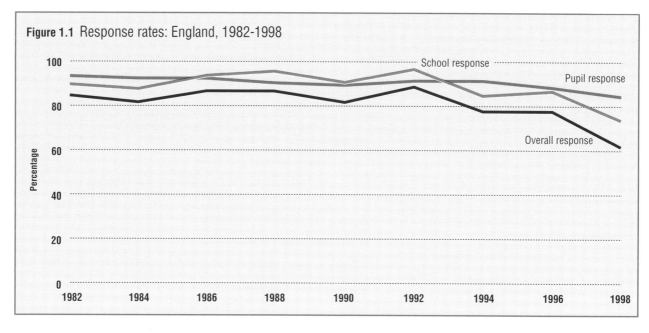

Figure 1.1 Response rates: England, 1982-1998

Whatever the reason for the poor response, it is important to attempt to assess its effect on the quality of the data, but unfortunately there is only limited data available with which to do this. There was no significant response variation between schools of different sizes or types (comprehensive, Grant Maintained, independent) nor according to whether mixed sex or single sex, but there was variation in response by region. The proportion of sampled schools taking part in the survey was highest in the North (81%) and the South (76%), but considerably lower in the Midlands (67%) and the Greater London area (61%). Although the difference in response rate is striking, the effect on the national data is likely to be small, because the proportion of the sample in Greater London, for example, is reduced by only a modest amount, from 13% of the set sample to 11% of the achieved sample. Thus there would need to be substantial non-response bias for the national data to be significantly affected. The available data provide no evidence of this, since the series of surveys has shown no consistent regional differences in smoking, but it cannot completely be ruled out, as it is known that there is considerable variation in behaviour from school to school which is not related to characteristics of the school such as type or size.

1.5 Reweighting of data

Because probabilities of selection varied according to school year, data have been reweighted to adjust for this.

The purpose of showing bases in tables is to enable the reader to judge the likely reliability of the data by inspection of the size of the base and to allow the calculation of sampling errors if required. To aid this, in tables where age or school year is a variable, the base shown for each age group is the number interviewed, rather than the reweighted figure (which would show more 11-13 year olds, for example, and fewer 14 and 15 year olds than actually took part in the survey). In these tables, the bases for individual years of age do not necessarily sum to the total shown, which is the reweighted figure.

1.6 Precision of estimates

Since the data presented in this report were obtained from a sample of school children, they are subject to sampling error, and this must be taken into account when considering the results. Any sample is only one of an almost infinite number that might have been selected, all producing slightly different estimates. Appendix A explains how to calculate sampling errors for the data shown in this report.

In general, attention is only drawn to differences between groups and between survey years if they are statistically significant at the 0.05 confidence level: that is, there is less than a 5% probability that the difference in question is due to random sampling fluctuation and no difference occurred in the population from which the sample was drawn.

It is important, however, to recognise that sampling error is only one of the sources of error which affect the accuracy of any survey results. Other sources of inaccuracy include over- and under-reporting and non-response bias (mentioned above).

References

1   Goddard E and Higgins V. *Smoking, drinking and drug use among young teenagers in 1998: Volume 2: Scotland*, 1999 (London: SO)

Table 1.1 Summary of response rates

	Saliva		Non-saliva		Total	
		%		%		%
Schools sampled	100	100	100	100	200	100
Co-operating schools	69	69	78	78	147	74
Number of pupils selected	2637	100	2961	100	5598	100
Pupils interviewed	2148	81	2604	88	4752	85
Total non-response	489	19	357	12	846	15
absent, sick	79	3	87	3	166	3
absent, truant	37	1	18	1	55	1
absent, reason unknown	149	6	99	3	248	4
refusal by pupil	36	1	22	1	58	1
refusal by parent	78	3	47	2	125	2
other	110	4	84	3	194	3
Overall response rate (allowing for non-response of schools and pupils)		56		69		62

2 Classification of smoking behaviour

2.1 Introduction

The classification of smoking behaviour used in this series of surveys is based on a combination of information from the self-completion questionnaire and the smoking diary. The intention of this classification is to distinguish between children who are regular smokers, even if infrequent ones, and those who are not. It is based on answers to the prevalence questions, except that those who say at the prevalence questions that they are not smokers but record cigarettes on the diary are classified as occasional smokers (irrespective of the number of cigarettes recorded).

Saliva testing for the presence of cotinine, which is a major metabolite of nicotine, was introduced in 1988 with a view to validating the estimates of the prevalence of smoking, and has been repeated in every survey since then. Results of the cotinine assay have consistently indicated that on the whole, children are honest about their smoking – only a handful of children in each survey have had saliva cotinine concentrations clearly at odds with their self-reported smoking behaviour. Saliva cotinine levels have not been used as a basis for re-classifying the smoking behaviour of individual children - and if they had, prevalence rates would not have been altered.

The relationship between the questionnaire, diary and cotinine information for individual children has been discussed in detail in earlier reports[1] and is not covered here. A section is, however, included on the effect of the cotinine testing on the estimates of the self-reported prevalence of smoking.

2.2 Smoking behaviour according to the questionnaire

The prevalence question is in two parts, a main question followed by a check question for those who say at the main question that they have never smoked, as shown in Figure 2.1. In each survey, a small proportion (7% in 1998) of those who initially say that they have never smoked admit at the check question that they have done so, and are reclassified accordingly. Table 2.1 shows that, in 1998, using the combined measure rather than just the first question reduces the proportion of pupils saying they have never smoked from 57% to 53%. The proportion who, at the date of the survey, had apparently experimented briefly with cigarettes rises from 16% to 20%.

(Figure 2.1, Table 2.1)

2.3 Cigarettes smoked according to the diary

In addition to the questionnaire, pupils also completed a diary covering the previous seven days. Each day was divided into six broad periods: early morning, morning, dinner time, afternoon, teatime and evening. For each period, for each of the previous seven days, pupils were asked a question about what they had been doing at that time, and were asked to record how many cigarettes, if any, they had smoked. All pupils were asked to complete the diary, whatever they had said about their smoking in answer to the prevalence question.

Table 2.2 shows the number of cigarettes recorded on the diary for pupils classified by their responses at the prevalence question. Complete consistency

Figure 2.1

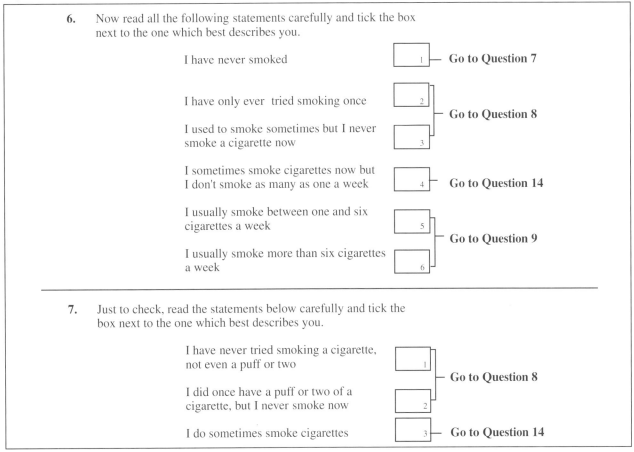

The following statements and questionnaire items are shown in Figure 2.1:

6. Now read all the following statements carefully and tick the box next to the one which best describes you.

I have never smoked [1] — **Go to Question 7**

I have only ever tried smoking once [2]
I used to smoke sometimes but I never smoke a cigarette now [3] — **Go to Question 8**

I sometimes smoke cigarettes now but I don't smoke as many as one a week [4] — **Go to Question 14**

I usually smoke between one and six cigarettes a week [5]
I usually smoke more than six cigarettes a week [6] — **Go to Question 9**

7. Just to check, read the statements below carefully and tick the box next to the one which best describes you.

I have never tried smoking a cigarette, not even a puff or two [1]
I did once have a puff or two of a cigarette, but I never smoke now [2] — **Go to Question 8**

I do sometimes smoke cigarettes [3] — **Go to Question 14**

between the two sets of answers would not be expected, because the prevalence questions asked about usual behaviour, whereas the diary related to what was smoked in the previous week. However, as in previous surveys, both regular and occasional smokers seem to have underestimated how much they smoked at the prevalence question. For example, 68% of those who said that they usually smoked between one and six cigarettes a week had recorded seven or more cigarettes on the diary as being smoked last week. Underestimation of consumption does not affect the classification of pupils as regular smokers, which depended only on their saying that they smoked at least one cigarette a week at the prevalence question.

However, similar under reporting seems to have occurred among those who said that they did smoke, but not as many as one a week. About one in five of this group (21%) had apparently smoked on average one or more cigarettes a day in the previous week. This suggests that some children who are probably regular smokers (according to the definition we are using) have been classified as occasional smokers.

(Table 2.2)

The inconsistencies noted between answers at the prevalence question and cigarettes recorded on the diary are in most cases unlikely to result from children deliberately giving inconsistent answers. Surveys of smoking among adults have found that they, too, underestimate cigarette consumption - there may be a natural tendency to do so, particularly when asked to estimate the number of cigarettes smoked over a period. In addition, some children may have had difficulty with the concepts of present and past behaviour underlying the prevalence question; these may tend to imply the more stable, settled pattern of adult life rather than the more erratic, experimental behaviour of some children.

The lack of correspondence between self-reported smoking on the questionnaire and the diary suggests that the 'occasional smoker' category is not a distinct one. At a period in children's lives when smoking behaviour is constantly changing the composition of this group is also very unstable.

The full classification of smoking behaviour, using both the questionnaire and the diary information, is shown in Table 2.3.

(Table 2.3)

2.4 The procedure used for obtaining saliva specimens

Saliva specimens were obtained from all pupils in half the sample of schools. Because of the effect of clustering in the sample design, it is not ideal to have all the pupils in one school allocated to either the saliva or the non-saliva sample, but this is more practicable than collecting specimens from half the pupils in each school.

The saliva specimens were obtained while pupils were filling in the questionnaires and diaries, and they were fully aware of the purpose of the procedure. They were given a small tube containing a dental roll, and asked to put the latter in the mouth between the cheek and the gum, and to leave it there without chewing it (which reduces the amount of saliva retained) while they filled in the questionnaire and the diary. After twenty minutes, they were told to take out the dental roll and put it back in the labelled tube. The specimens were subsequently sent to the Health Behaviour Unit at the University College London Medical School for analysis by gas chromatography.

Cotinine is a major metabolite of nicotine. It has a half-life in saliva of 16-20 hours, and so reflects exposure to tobacco smoke over the past few days. In the remainder of this chapter, the effect of the cotinine testing on the estimates of the prevalence of smoking is discussed.

2.5 The effects of the saliva test on estimates of the prevalence of smoking

A priori, it might be expected that saliva testing would, if anything, encourage pupils to be more honest, and increase the proportion of pupils reporting on the questionnaire that they were smokers.

The first time the procedure was used, in the 1988 survey, the saliva test did seem to have an effect on self-reported prevalence, but from 1990 to 1994 there were no significant differences between the test and control samples. In 1996, however, the reported prevalence of cigarette smoking was higher in the test sample than in the control sample, and the same was the case in 1998. In 1998, 12% of the test group reported that they were regular smokers compared with 10% of the control group, and the difference is just statistically significant at the 95% level. There was also a difference in the proportion reporting that they had never smoked - 50% of the test group and 55% of the control group said they had never smoked. These differences between the test and control groups were evident among both boys and girls.

As the series of surveys have not consistently shown a significant difference in prevalence between the saliva test and control groups, the differences in 1996 and 1998 may have been due to slight variations in the characteristics of the two samples rather than to the test itself. Although the splitting of the sample of schools was controlled, so that the subsamples were well matched, it was not possible to control the number of boys and girls selected in each school, and some differences between the test and control samples would be expected, simply from random sampling variation. For example, those in the test sample were slightly older on average than those in the control sample, which would tend to increase overall prevalence among those tested relative to those not tested.

(Tables 2.4-2.5)

References

1   For the most recent discussion, see Appendix B in Jarvis L *Smoking among secondary school children in 1996: England 1997* (London: The Stationery Office)

Table 2.1 Replies to prevalence and check question

All pupils   *England 1998*

	Prevalence question	Check question	Both questions combined
	%	%	%
I have never smoked	57	93	53
I have only smoked once	16	7	20
I used to smoke sometimes, but I never smoke now	12	0	12
I sometimes smoke cigarettes now, but I don't smoke as many as one a week	5	0	5
I usually smoke between one and six cigarettes a week	3	0	3
I usually smoke more than six cigarettes a week	7	0	7
Base (=100%)	4725	2660	4725

Table 2.2 Cigarettes recorded on the diary, by smoking behaviour according to the questionnaire

All pupils   *England 1998*

Cigarettes on diary	Usually smokes: more than 6 a week	1-6 a week	less than 1 a week	Used to smoke	Tried smoking	Never smoked	Total
	%	%	%	%	%	%	%
None	2	6	38	85	95	100	84
1-6	2	27	42	10	5	0	5
7-70	52	64	19	4	1	0	8
71 or more	45	4	2	0	0	0	4
Base (=100%)	*343*	*159*	*235*	*548*	*935*	*2497*	*4717*

Table 2.3 Classification of smoking behaviour derived from the questionnaire and the diary

England 1998

Classification	Smoking prevalence question	Diary	Number of pupils	%
Regular smoker	usually smokes more than 6 cigs	cigs	338 ⎫	
	usually smokes more than 6 cigs	no cigs	5 ⎬ 501	11
	usually smokes 1-6 cigs	cigs	149	
	usually smokes 1-6 cigs	no cigs	9 ⎭	
Occasional smoker	smokes sometimes	cigs	145 ⎫	
	smokes sometimes	no cigs	89	
	used to smoke	cigs	80 ⎬ 373	8
	tried smoking once	cigs	50	
	never smoked	cigs	9 ⎭	
Used to smoke	used to smoke	no cigs	468	10
Tried smoking once	tried smoking once	no cigs	885	19
Never smoked	never smoked	no cigs	2488	53
Total			4715	

Table 2.4 Smoking behaviour by sex and whether in test or control sample

All pupils   *England 1998*

	Boys		Girls		Total	
Smoking behaviour	Test	Control	Test	Control	Test	Control
	%	%	%	%	%	%
Regular smoker	10	8	14	11	12	10
Occasional smoker	8	7	8	8	8	8
Used to smoke	10	9	11	10	10	10
Tried smoking once	22	18	17	18	19	18
Never smoked	50	58	50	52	50	55
Base (=100%)	*1079*	*1234*	*1083*	*1330*	*2161*	*2565*

Table 2.5 Smoking prevalence by sex and whether in test or control sample: 1988-1998

All pupils   *England*

	Boys		Girls		Total	
Survey year	Test	Control	Test	Control	Test	Control
			Percentage who were regular smokers			
1988	8	6	11	6	10	6
1990	11	12	13	12	12	12
1992	8	10	10	10	9	10
1994	9	11	14	12	12	12
1996	13	9	16	14	14	11
1998	10	8	14	11	12	10
1998 base (=100%)	*1079*	*1234*	*1083*	*1330*	*2161*	*2565*

3 Smoking prevalence and consumption

3.1 **Trends in the prevalence of cigarette smoking**

This series of surveys has been monitoring changes in the prevalence of cigarette smoking among secondary school children biennially since 1982, and over that period, there has been some fluctuation.

In 1998, the overall prevalence of smoking among 11-15 year olds was 11%, compared with 13% in 1996. Continuing the pattern first established in the mid-1980s, prevalence was significantly higher among girls (12%) than among boys (9%).

Changes in prevalence among school children have been reasonably consistent with those among young adults established by the General Household Survey, although the measures used are not exactly the same[1]. Between 1982 and 1996, the prevalence of smoking among 16-19 year olds, as established by the GHS, ranged between 27% and 31%, with no clear increasing or decreasing trend over that period. Among children, if the exceptionally low figure of 8% in 1988 is discounted, prevalence over the same period has ranged between 10% and 13%, again, with no apparent long-term pattern of change. So although the fall in prevalence between 1996 and 1998 is statistically significant, it may just represent a short term fluctuation, rather than the start of a downward trend.

It was noted in Chapter 1 that Social Survey Division of ONS also carried out a series of three surveys for the Health Education Authority in 1996, 1997, and 1998. Although the main purpose of these surveys was to look at attitudes to smoking and anti-smoking campaigns,

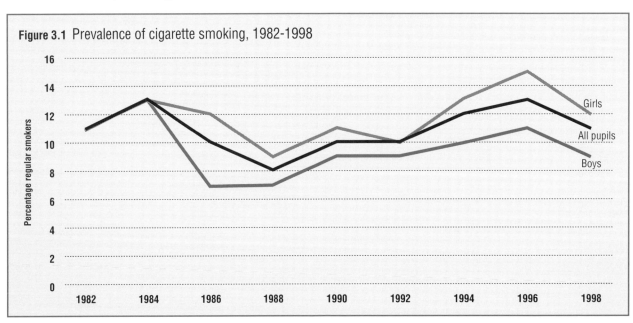

Figure 3.1 Prevalence of cigarette smoking, 1982-1998

information about smoking behaviour was collected to provide a context for consideration of the other topics. Over the series of three surveys, prevalence has been remarkably constant at 10% or 11% (and was unaffected by the taking of saliva specimens in 1997 and 1998, but not in 1996).

(Figure 3.1, Table 3.1)

3.2 **Smoking behaviour in relation to age and school year**

Earlier reports in this series have shown that the likelihood of a boy or girl smoking grows with age and progress through the school (these two factors being, of course, closely linked), and that of the two, age is the more important factor. These earlier analyses are confirmed by the data presented in Figure 3.2, in which pupils at each year of age are divided into three-month age cohorts. The proportion of pupils who have ever smoked rises fairly steadily over the whole age range, rather than in a series of sharp increases from one school year to the next.

Very few pupils are smokers when they start secondary school: among children aged 11 in 1998, only 1% were regular smokers, and four in five had never even tried smoking. By the age of 15, however, 24% of pupils were regular smokers, and only 30% had never tried a cigarette.

Among both boys and girls aged 15, the prevalence of smoking was lower in 1998 than in 1996. In 1998, among 15 year-olds, almost three

in ten girls were regular smokers, compared with about two in ten boys of the same age. Differences in prevalence between boys and girls were also evident among those aged 13 and 14.

(Figure 3.2, Tables 3.2-3.5)

3.3 **Regional variation in smoking behaviour**

Regional variations in smoking behaviour are difficult to interpret because, even with the larger sample in 1998, the sample size in each region is still small. This in itself leads to relatively high sampling errors, which are further increased by the fact that the sample is clustered in schools. The problem is partially overcome by grouping the regions into four larger areas[2]; the North, the Midlands (and Wales prior to 1988) the South, and Greater London, but even so, the sample in Greater London was clustered in only 15 schools.

In 1998, prevalence was higher in the South than in the North (12% compared with 10%) reversing the 1996 picture. Indeed, it can be seen from Table 3.6 that the surveys have shown no consistent pattern of regional variation in smoking behaviour during the 16 year period in which they have been carried out. There was a statistically significant decrease in the North from 15% in 1996 to 10% in 1998 - back to the same level as in 1994. There was also a decrease in prevalence in Greater London from 13% of pupils in 1996 to 8% in 1998.

(Figure 3.3, Table 3.6)

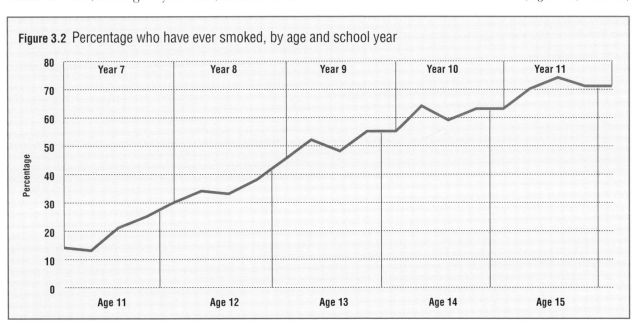

Figure 3.2 Percentage who have ever smoked, by age and school year

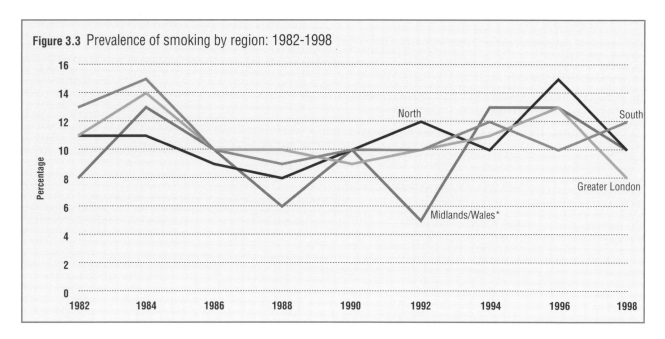

Figure 3.3 Prevalence of smoking by region: 1982-1998

3.4 **Cigarette consumption according to the diary**

Cigarette consumption was measured by summing the number of cigarettes recorded on the diary as being smoked on each day of the previous week.

The majority of regular smokers, 71%, had recorded more than 20 cigarettes in the diary: indeed almost one third had recorded more than seventy a week, (an average of at least ten cigarettes a day. Only 3% of regular smokers had not smoked in the previous week, compared with 24% of occasional smokers. One half of all occasional smokers had smoked between one and five cigarettes during the diary week. Two per cent of those who said they were occasional smokers had recorded smoking on average at least ten cigarettes a day.

Among regular smokers, boys were much more likely than girls to have smoked at least ten cigarettes a day: 38% of boys who were regular smokers, but only 27% of girls, had done so.

Table 3.7 also shows the mean numbers of cigarettes recorded by regular and occasional smokers. These averages are based on all regular and occasinal smokers, including those who recorded no cigarettes on the diary. The median number of cigarettes is also presented, since a few pupils record a large number of cigarettes on the diary, and this has a disproportionate influence on the mean value.

Reflecting the much higher proportion of boys than of girls who were smoking at least ten cigarettes a day, mean consumption was much higher among boys than among girls: among regular smokers, boys had smoked an average of 65 cigarettes in the previous week, compared with 49 for girls. Among occasional smokers, too, boys' consumption was higher than that of girls.

(Table 3.7)

3.5 **Trends in cigarette consumption**

The pattern of cigarette consumption has remained broadly the same since the survey began, despite changes in prevalence levels, but in 1998 there was an increase in mean consumption among regular smokers to 56 cigarettes a week from around 50 a week in 1992, 1994 and 1996. This was largely due to an increase in consumption among boys from an average of 56 cigarettes a week in 1996 to an average of 65 in 1998.

Most of this series of surveys have shown that, although girls are more likely than boys to be regular smokers, among those who do smoke, boys smoke more cigarettes in an average week. The mean number of cigarettes smoked per pupil has remained fairly constant at around six or seven cigarettes a week (except in 1988, which, as has been noted earlier, seems to have been an atypical year).

(Table 3.8)

Notes and references

1   This survey defines a regular smoker as someone who usually smokes at least once cigarette a week, whereas on the GHS, a smoker is someone who 'smokes cigarettes at all nowadays'.

2   The four broad regions are as follows:

North	North, Yorkshire & Humberside, North West
Midlands	East Midlands, West Midlands, East Anglia (and Wales in 1982, 1984 and 1986)
South	South East, South West
Greater London	

Table 3.1 Smoking behaviour by sex: 1982 to 1998

All pupils *England*

Smoking behaviour	1982	1984	1986	1988	1990	1992	1994	1996	1998
Boys	%	%	%	%	%	%	%	%	%
Regular smoker	11	13	7	7	9	9	10	11	9
Occasional smoker	7	9	5	5	6	6	9	8	8
Used to smoke	11	11	10	8	7	6	7	7	9
Tried smoking	26	24	23	23	22	22	21	22	20
Never smoked	45	44	55	58	56	57	53	53	54
Base(=100%)	*1460*	*1928*	*1676*	*1489*	*1643*	*1662*	*1522*	*1445*	*2311*
Girls	%	%	%	%	%	%	%	%	%
Regular smoker	11	13	12	9	11	10	13	15	12
Occasional smoker	9	9	5	5	6	7	10	10	8
Used to smoke	10	10	10	9	7	7	8	9	10
Tried smoking	22	22	19	19	18	19	17	18	18
Never smoked	49	46	53	59	58	57	52	48	51
Base(=100%)	*1514*	*1689*	*1508*	*1529*	*1478*	*1626*	*1523*	*1409*	*2413*
Total	%	%	%	%	%	%	%	%	%
Regular smoker	11	13	10	8	10	10	12	13	11
Occasional smoker	8	9	5	5	6	7	9	9	8
Used to smoke	10	10	10	8	7	7	8	8	10
Tried smoking	24	23	21	21	20	20	19	20	19
Never smoked	47	45	54	58	57	57	53	51	53
Base(=100%)	*2979*	*3658*	*3189*	*3018*	*3121*	*3295*	*3045*	*2854*	*4723*

Table 3.2 Smoking behaviour by sex and age

All pupils   *England 1998*

Smoking behaviour	11 years	12 years	13 years	14 years	15 years	Total
	%	%	%	%	%	%
Boys						
Regular smoker	1	3	5	15	19	9
Occasional smoker	3	7	8	8	11	8
Used to smoke	3	5	12	11	15	9
Tried smoking	16	18	21	23	21	20
Never smoked	78	67	54	42	34	54
Base(=100%)	*300*	*349*	*302*	*612*	*754*	*2317*
	%	%	%	%	%	%
Girls						
Regular smoker	1	3	9	19	29	12
Occasional smoker	3	6	9	13	11	8
Used to smoke	2	7	13	13	16	10
Tried smoking	12	18	21	17	18	18
Never smoked	82	66	48	37	26	51
Base(=100%)	*303*	*375*	*390*	*670*	*673*	*2411*
	%	%	%	%	%	%
Total						
Regular smoker	1	3	7	17	24	11
Occasional smoker	3	6	9	11	11	8
Used to smoke	2	6	13	12	15	10
Tried smoking	14	18	21	20	20	19
Never smoked	80	67	50	40	30	53
Base(=100%)	*603*	*724*	*692*	*1282*	*1427*	*4728*

Table 3.3 Smoking behaviour by sex and school year

All pupils   *England 1998*

Smoking behaviour	Year 7	Year 8	Year 9	Year 10	Year 11	Total
	%	%	%	%	%	%
Boys						
Regular smoker	1	3	5	17	20	9
Occasional smoker	3	7	8	9	11	8
Used to smoke	2	6	12	11	16	9
Tried smoking	14	20	23	23	20	20
Never smoked	79	64	52	40	34	54
Base(=100%)	*338*	*359*	*300*	*667*	*651*	*2315*
	%	%	%	%	%	%
Girls						
Regular smoker	1	4	10	21	29	12
Occasional smoker	3	6	10	13	11	8
Used to smoke	2	8	13	14	16	10
Tried smoking	13	19	21	16	18	18
Never smoked	81	64	46	36	25	51
Base(=100%)	*347*	*385*	*394*	*685*	*602*	*2413*
	%	%	%	%	%	%
Total						
Regular smoker	1	4	8	19	24	11
Occasional smoker	3	6	9	11	11	8
Used to smoke	2	7	12	12	16	10
Tried smoking	14	20	22	20	19	19
Never smoked	80	64	48	38	30	53
Base(=100%)	*685*	*744*	*694*	*1352*	*1253*	*4728*

Table 3.4 Proportion of pupils who were regular smokers by sex and age; 1982 to 1998

All pupils   *England*

Age	1982	1984	1986	1988	1990	1992	1994	1996	1998	*1998 base (=100%)*
					Percentage who were regular smokers					
Boys										
aged 11	1	0	0	0	0	0	1	1	1	*300*
aged 12	2	2	2	2	2	2	2	2	3	*349*
aged 13	8	10	5	5	6	6	4	8	5	*302*
aged 14	18	16	6	8	10	14	14	13	15	*612*
aged 15	24	28	18	17	25	21	26	28	19	*754*
Total	11	13	7	7	9	9	10	11	9	*2317*
Girls										
aged 11	0	1	0	1	1	0	0	0	1	*303*
aged 12	1	2	2	0	2	2	3	4	3	*375*
aged 13	6	9	5	4	9	9	8	11	9	*390*
aged 14	14	19	16	12	16	15	20	24	19	*670*
aged 15	25	28	27	22	25	25	30	33	29	*673*
Total	11	13	12	9	11	10	13	15	12	*2411*

Table 3.5 Proportion of pupils who were regular smokers by sex and school year: 1982 to 1998

All pupils   *England*

School year	1982	1984	1986	1988	1990	1992	1994	1996	1998	*1998 base (=100%)*
					Percentage who were regular smokers					
Boys										
year 7	3	0	0	1	1	1	2	1	1	*338*
year 8	2	3	2	2	3	3	2	4	3	*359*
year 9	9	12	5	5	7	7	5	8	5	*300*
year 10	19	17	8	9	12	16	15	13	17	*667*
year 11	26	31	19	18	26	20	28	28	20	*651*
Total	11	13	7	7	9	9	10	11	9	*2315*
Girls										
year 7	0	1	0	0	1	1	1	1	1	*347*
year 8	2	2	2	0	4	3	3	4	4	*385*
year 9	7	9	6	5	10	10	10	13	10	*394*
year 10	15	24	18	13	15	17	23	24	21	*685*
year 11	28	28	30	23	27	25	30	34	29	*602*
Total	11	13	12	9	11	10	13	15	12	*2413*

Table 3.6 Smoking behaviour by region: 1982 to 1998

All pupils   *England*

Region	1982	1984	1986	1988	1990	1992	1994	1996	1998
Regular smokers (%)									
North	11	11	9	8	10	12	10	15	10
Midlands/Wales*	8	13	10	6	10	5	13	13	10
South	13	15	10	9	10	10	12	10	12
Greater London	11	14	10	10	9	10	11	13	8
Occasional smokers (%)									
North	6	7	5	4	6	6	9	8	7
Midlands/Wales*	7	8	4	4	4	7	8	8	8
South	11	11	6	6	8	7	10	10	10
Greater London	5	7	7	7	7	8	9	8	8
Used to smoke (%)									
North	10	11	9	10	7	7	6	10	10
Midlands/Wales*	8	9	11	8	7	6	10	8	10
South	12	11	11	8	6	7	8	8	9
Greater London	13	11	8	6	9	4	6	6	12
Tried smoking once (%)									
North	23	23	20	19	20	20	22	20	18
Midlands/Wales*	23	24	22	20	20	20	15	18	17
South	25	24	21	21	19	21	19	20	20
Greater London	23	22	19	27	24	22	20	22	20
Has never smoked (%)									
North	50	49	57	60	57	55	52	48	55
Midlands/Wales*	53	46	53	62	59	63	54	53	55
South	38	39	52	57	56	56	52	51	49
Greater London	48	45	56	50	52	56	53	51	52
Bases (=100%)									
North	*966*	*1092*	*910*	*929*	*1072*	*1020*	*939*	*885*	*1691*
*Midlands/Wales**	*834*	*1061*	*910*	*772*	*805*	*807*	*670*	*732*	*1097*
South	*932*	*1114*	*1034*	*991*	*988*	*1102*	*1075*	*890*	*1499*
Greater London	*247*	*389*	*338*	*354*	*256*	*366*	*361*	*347*	*438*

* Wales was part of the England and Wales sample in 1982, 1984 and 1986.
From 1988 onwards, figures are for the Midlands only

Table 3.7 Number of cigarettes smoked in the previous seven days, by sex

Current smokers   *England 1998*

Cigarette consumption	Boys	Girls	Total
Regular smokers	%	%	%
None	4	2	3
1-5	5	11	8
6-10	4	6	5
11-20	8	14	11
21-70	41	40	40
71 or more	38	27	31
Mean	65	49	56
Median	55	41	46
Occasional smokers	%	%	%
None	24	24	24
1-5	47	54	50
6-10	10	10	10
11-20	8	6	7
21-70	8	6	6
71 or more	3	1	2
Mean	11	6	8
Median	2	2	2
All smokers	%	%	%
None	13	11	12
1-5	24	28	26
6-10	7	8	7
11-20	8	11	10
21-70	26	26	26
71 or more	22	16	19
Mean	41	31	35
Median	16	13	14
Base(=100%)			
Regular smokers	*207*	*295*	*502*
Occasional smokers	*174*	*201*	*375*
All smokers	*381*	*496*	*877*

Table 3.8 Mean and median cigarette consumption in the diary week by sex: 1982 to 1998

All pupils *England*

Region	1982	1984	1986	1988	1990	1992	1994	1996	1998
Boys									
Regular smokers									
Mean	50	49	53	52	56	58	54	56	65
Median	40	40	43	49	48	51	44	46	55
Occasional smokers									
Mean	7	5	5	7	7	6	7	8	11
Median	2	1	1	3	3	1	2	3	2
Mean consumption per pupil	6	7	4	4	6	5	6	7	7
Girls									
Regular smokers									
Mean	44	49	45	41	49	44	47	47	49
Median	36	38	36	38	40	34	37	40	41
Occasional smokers									
Mean	4	4	4	4	4	3	3	5	6
Median	1	2	1	1	2	1	2	2	2
Mean consumption per pupil	5	7	6	4	5	4	6	8	6
Total									
Regular smokers									
Mean	47	49	48	46	53	51	50	51	56
Median	38	39	38	41	43	42	39	44	46
Occasional smokers									
Mean	6	4	5	6	6	5	5	7	8
Median	1	1	1	1	2	1	2	2	2
Mean consumption per pupil	6	7	5	4	6	5	6	7	7
Bases (=100%)									
Boys									
Regular smokers	166	251	123	107	148	134	147	154	207
Occasional smokers	106	168	88	70	98	96	138	107	174
All pupils	1460	1928	1676	1488	1640	1641	1515	1442	2311
Girls									
Regular smokers	159	221	183	136	158	147	200	208	295
Occasional smokers	130	152	82	76	90	96	143	141	201
All pupils	1514	1689	1508	1529	1478	1597	1521	1408	2413
Total									
Regular smokers	326	474	306	246	306	281	347	362	502
Occasional smokers	236	324	170	148	188	192	281	248	375
All pupils	2979	3658	3189	3017	3118	3245	3036	2850	4723

4 Dependence on smoking

4.1 Length of time as a smoker

Regular smokers were asked how long it was since they started smoking at least one cigarette a week. In 1998, almost two-thirds, 65%, said that they had been doing so for more than one year: this was similar to the 67% of regular smokers who had been smoking for more than one year in 1996.

(Table 4.1)

4.2 Dependence on smoking

Regular smokers were asked a series of questions designed to give some indication of whether or not they were dependent on smoking. Fifty-eight per cent of regular smokers felt that it would be difficult to go without smoking for a week, half of whom said that they would find it very difficult. Almost three in four regular

smokers said that they would find it difficult to give up smoking altogether. Although a higher proportion of girls than of boys reported that they would find it difficult to give up (74% compared with 67%), this difference was not statistically significant.

In 1998, 35% of regular smokers said they would like to give up smoking compared with 45% in 1996.

Forty per cent of regular smokers who had tried to give up smoking would still like to give up, but 14% said that they definitely would not like to try again - perhaps because of their lack of success in the past. However, those who had tried to give up were still about twice as likely to want to give up as were those who had not tried (40% compared with 21%).

(Tables 4.2-4.5)

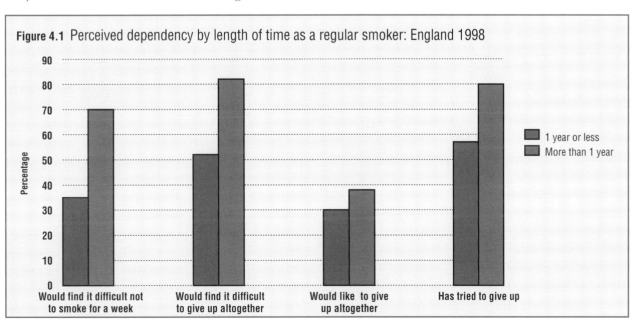

Figure 4.1 Perceived dependency by length of time as a regular smoker: England 1998

Smokers who had been smoking regularly for more than a year were much more likely to feel dependent than were those who had started smoking more recently, but even among the latter group, just over half said that they would find it difficult to give up altogether.

It may be that the longer pupils have smoked, the more likely they are to have a realistic assessment of the difficulty of giving up, and the more likely they are to have tried to give up and failed (80% of longer term smokers had tried to give up compared with 57% of those smoking for one year or less).

There was also a difference between those who had been smoking regularly for more than a year and those who had smoked for a shorter time in the proportions who said they would like to give up smoking (38% compared with 30%).

(Figure 4.1, Table 4.6)

As discussed in previous reports, the results of this survey suggest that girls may be dependent on smoking (or may think they are) at lower levels of nicotine intake. For example, girls who reported they would find it difficult not to smoke for a week smoked on average 66 cigarettes a week compared with an average of 86 cigarettes smoked by boys giving the same answer.

(Tables 4.7-4.8)

4.3 Attitudes of the family towards pupils' smoking

Current smokers were asked how their families felt about their smoking. They were also given the opportunity to say that their family did not know they smoked. Although all these questions referred to the feelings of the family, it is likely that children were thinking primarily of their parents when they answered them.

Thirty-five per cent of current smokers said that their families tried to stop them smoking or encouraged them not to smoke. Only 11% said that their families did not mind that they smoked. However, 44% of all current smokers thought that their families did not know they smoked. Previous surveys have consistently shown that girls are much more likely than boys to keep their smoking secret from their families.

This was also the case in 1998 - 40% of boys and 47% of girls thought that their families did not know they smoked - although the difference was not statistically significant.

Occasional smokers were almost twice as likely as were regular smokers to say that their families did not know they smoked - 66% compared with 35%.

Regular smokers were more than twice as likely as occasional smokers to say their family encouraged them not to smoke (37% of regular smokers compared with 16% of occasional smokers), and 15% of regular smokers, compared with only 3% of occasional smokers, said that their family did not mind them smoking.

Seventeen per cent of current smokers were allowed to smoke at home if they wanted to.

(Tables 4.9-4.11)

Table 4.1 Length of time as a regular smoker, by sex: 1988 to 1998

Regular smokers   *England*

Length of time as a regular smoker	1988	1990	1992	1994	1996	1998
	%	%	%	%	%	%
Boys						
Less than 3 months	11	8	17	13	7	10
3-6 months	14	14	14	8	5	5
6 months to 1 year	21	16	12	19	19	18
More than 1 year	54	62	57	61	69	67
Base(=100%)	*106*	*146*	*143*	*150*	*150*	*198*
	%	%	%	%	%	%
Girls						
Less than 3 months	10	11	11	11	10	10
3-6 months	11	13	18	13	9	8
6 months to 1 year	21	23	14	22	16	18
More than 1 year	57	53	57	54	65	64
Base(=100%)	*134*	*153*	*162*	*195*	*198*	*277*
	%	%	%	%	%	%
Total						
Less than 3 months	11	9	14	12	9	10
3-6 months	13	14	16	11	7	6
6 months to 1 year	21	19	13	20	18	18
More than 1 year	55	58	57	57	67	65
Base(=100%)	*243*	*299*	*305*	*345*	*348*	*475*

Table 4.2 Whether regular smokers would find it easy or difficult not to smoke for a week by sex: 1994 to 1998

Regular smokers   *England*

Difficulty or ease of not smoking for a week	1994		1996		1998	
		%		%		%
Boys						
Very difficult	}54	19	}66	33	}54	31
Fairly difficult		34		33		23
Fairly easy	}46	30	}34	24	}46	29
Very easy		16		10		17
Base (=100%)	*148*		*150*		*199*	
		%		%		%
Girls						
Very difficult	}61	24	}64	31	}60	28
Fairly difficult		37		33		32
Fairly easy	}39	27	}36	26	}40	29
Very easy		12		10		11
Base (=100%)	*195*		*199*		*276*	
		%		%		%
Total						
Very difficult	}58	22	}65	32	}58	29
Fairly difficult		36		33		28
Fairly easy	}42	28	}35	25	}42	29
Very easy		14		10		13
Base (=100%)	*343*		*349*		*475*	

Table 4.3 Whether regular smokers would find it easy or difficult to give up smoking altogether, by sex: 1994 to 1998

Regular smokers   *England*

Difficulty or ease of giving up altogether	1994		1996		1998	
	%		%		%	
Boys						
Very difficult	30	}66	43	}76	37	}67
Fairly difficult	36		33		30	
Fairly easy	22	}34	17	}24	25	}33
Very easy	12		7		8	
Base (=100%)	*148*		*150*		*199*	
	%		%		%	
Girls						
Very difficult	38	}73	44	}75	36	}74
Fairly difficult	35		31		38	
Fairly easy	20	}27	21	}25	21	}26
Very easy	7		5		5	
Base (=100%)	*195*		*199*		*276*	
	%		%		%	
Total						
Very difficult	35	}70	44	}75	36	}72
Fairly difficult	35		32		35	
Fairly easy	21	}30	19	}25	22	}29
Very easy	9		6		6	
Base (=100%)	*343*		*349*		*475*	

Table 4.4 Whether regular smokers (a) would like to give up smoking altogether (b) have ever tried to give up smoking by sex: 1994-1998

Regular smokers *England*

	1994	1996	1998
Boys			
Would like to give up	%	%	%
Yes	36	45	38
No	20	21	22
Don't know	44	33	40
Percentage who have tried to give up	52	67	69
Base (=100%)	*149*	*150*	*199*
Girls			
Would like to give up	%	%	%
Yes	33	44	32
No	18	9	16
Don't know	49	47	52
Percentage who have tried to give up	70	80	74
Base (=100%)	*195*	*199*	*277*
Total	%	%	%
Would like to give up			
Yes	34	45	35
No	19	14	18
Don't know	47	41	47
Percentage who have tried to give up	62	75	72
Base (=100%)	*344*	*349*	*476*

Table 4.5 Whether regular smokers would like to give up by whether they have tried, by sex

Regular smokers *England 1998*

Whether would like to give up	Whether has ever tried to give up		
	Yes	No	Total
	%	%	%
Boys			
Yes	44	24	38
No	15	36	22
Don't know	40	40	40
	%	%	%
Girls			
Yes	37	19	32
No	14	23	16
Don't know	49	58	51
	%	%	%
Total			
Yes	40	21	35
No	14	29	18
Don't know	46	50	47
Base (=100%)			
Boys	*137*	*62*	*199*
Girls	*204*	*73*	*277*
Total	*340*	*136*	*476*

Table 4.6 Perceived dependency on smoking by sex and length of time as a regular smoker

Regular smokers *England 1998*

Dependency	Length of time as a smoker	
	1 year or less	More than one year
	Percentages	
Boys		
Would find it difficult not to smoke for a week	31	65
Would find it difficult to give up altogether	48	77
Would like to give up altogether	34	40
Has tried to give up	54	77
Base (=100%)	*64*	*133*
Girls		
Would find it difficult not to smoke for a week	38	73
Would find it difficult to give up altogether	55	85
Would like to give up altogether	26	37
Has tried to give up	58	82
Base (=100%)	*101*	*176*
Total		
Would find it difficult not to smoke for a week	35	70
Would find it difficult to give up altogether	52	82
Would like to give up altogether	30	38
Has tried to give up	57	80
Base (=100%)	*166*	*309*

Table 4.7 Mean number of cigarettes smoked in the previous seven days by sex and whether not smoking for a week would be easy or difficult

Regular smokers *England 1998*

Difficulty or ease of not smoking for a week	Boys	Girls	Total
	Mean number of cigarettes		
Difficult	86	66	74
Easy	42	25	33
All regular smokers	66	50	56
Bases			
Difficult	*105*	*166*	*271*
Easy	*91*	*110*	*201*
All regular smokers	*196*	*276*	*472*

Table 4.8 Mean number of cigarettes smoked in the previous seven days by sex and whether it would be easy or difficult to give up smoking altogether

Regular smokers *England 1998*

Difficulty or ease of giving up smoking altogether	Boys	Girls	Total
	Mean number of cigarettes		
Difficult	78	59	67
Easy	40	21	30
All regular smokers	66	49	56
Bases			
Difficult	*132*	*206*	*338*
Easy	*65*	*71*	*136*
All regular smokers	*197*	*278*	*475*

Table 4.9 Attitude of family to pupil's smoking, by sex*

Current smokers   *England 1998*

Attitude of family	Boys	Girls	Total
	%	%	%
Family:			
try to stop me	6	5	5
persuade me not to	31	30	30
don't mind	12	11	11
Don't know	11	7	9
They don't know I smoke	40	47	44
Base (=100%)	*311*	*409*	*720*

* Excludes pupils who were classified as occasional smokers
but who were self-reported non-smokers on the questionnaire

Table 4.10 Perceived attitude of family among current smokers by sex and smoking behaviour*

Current smokers   *England 1998*

Attitude of family	Regular smokers	Occasional smokers	All smokers
	%	%	%
Boys			
Family:	%	%	%
try to stop me	5	9	6
persuade me not to	38	18	31
don't mind	16	2	12
Don't know	9	14	11
They don't know I smoke	31	57	40
Girls			
Family:	%	%	%
try to stop me	5	3	5
persuade me not to	36	16	30
don't mind	15	2	11
Don't know	8	6	7
They don't know I smoke	37	73	47
Total			
Family:	%	%	%
try to stop me	5	6	5
persuade me not to	37	16	30
don't mind	15	3	11
Don't know	8	10	9
They don't know I smoke	35	66	44
Bases(=100%)			
Boys	*207*	*105*	*312*
Girls	*288*	*121*	*409*
Total	*495*	*226*	*720*

* Excludes pupils who were classified as occasional smokers but who were self-reported
non-smokers on the questionnaire

Table 4.11 Whether pupils are allowed to smoke at home, by sex

Current smokers   *England 1998*

Whether allowed to smoke at home	Boys	Girls	Total
	%	%	%
Yes	17	16	17
No	68	74	71
Don't know	15	9	12
Base (=100%)	*311*	*414*	*725*

5 Where children get their cigarettes

5.1 **Cigarette purchase in the last year**

Although it is illegal for cigarettes to be sold to children under the age of 16 (whether they are buying them for themselves or for an adult), previous surveys in the series have shown that many children do successfully buy cigarettes over the counter. The Children and Young Persons (Protection from Tobacco) Act 1991 greatly increased the penalties for the sale of tobacco to persons under the age of 16. The Act also made it illegal for shopkeepers to sell unpackaged cigarettes and required warning statements to be displayed in all retail premises and on cigarette vending machines.

Since 1986 the proportion of children trying to buy cigarettes from a shop has varied only from 25% to 27% (apart from in 1990 when a figure of 32% was recorded) but in 1998 it fell to 22%, the lowest level in the series of surveys. The proportion of boys and girls who were refused at least once in the last year when attempting to buy cigarettes from a shop rose from 38% in 1996 to its highest level , 43%, in 1998.

As might be expected given that the prevalence of smoking increases with age, the proportion of children trying to buy cigarettes increased from 4% of pupils aged 11 to 47% of those aged 15.

In 1998, a slightly higher proportion of boys than girls were refused by shopkeepers (44% compared with 42%) although the difference was not statistically significant. This continues the pattern shown in most previous surveys, apart from in 1996 when a higher proportion of girls than boys were refused. Generally, younger children were more likely to be refused cigarettes than older children. For example, 53% of 12 year

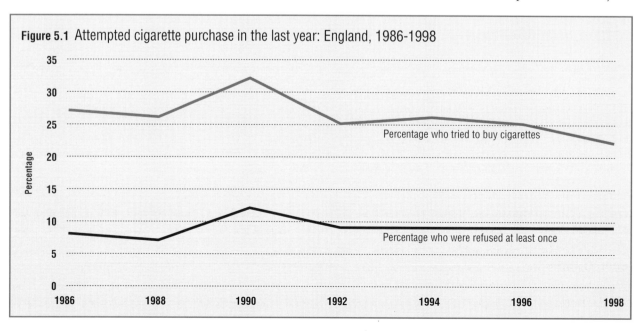

Figure 5.1 Attempted cigarette purchase in the last year: England, 1986-1998

Percentage who tried to buy cigarettes

Percentage who were refused at least once

olds who had attempted to buy cigarettes were refused at least once compared with 36% of 15 year olds.

(Figure 5.1, Tables 5.1-5.2)

5.2 Last time children tried to buy cigarettes from a shop

As well as being asked if they had been refused cigarettes in a shop at any time in the last year, pupils were also asked what had happened the last time they tried to buy cigarettes.

Fourteen per cent of pupils were refused the last time they tried to buy cigarettes in a shop. Not surprisingly, younger children were more likely than older children to have been refused - 38% of 11 and 12 year olds, but only 6% of 15 year olds were refused the last time they tried to buy cigarettes from a shop.

Current smokers were also less likely to have been refused on their last attempt to buy cigarettes than those who had never smoked - 9% of regular smokers were refused compared with 22% of those who had never smoked. This could partly be explained by the association between smoking behaviour and age (those who have never tried smoking tend to be younger) but it is also possible that smokers are more likely to know which shops will sell them cigarettes and which ones are likely to refuse them.

(Tables 5.3-5.4)

5.3 Who were the cigarettes bought for

The last time children purchased cigarettes in a shop, over half (52%) were buying them for themselves, about one third of pupils (34%) said they were buying them for a friend, and about one in ten (11%) said they were buying them for their parents.

Of those children who had bought cigarettes the last time they tried to do so, older children and regular smokers were most likely to have bought cigarettes for themselves, whereas younger children and non-smokers were most likely to have purchased cigarettes for their parents or for friends. For example, 53% of 15 year-olds had bought the cigarettes for themselves, but only 8%

had bought them for their parents. Almost one half of the pupils who had bought cigarettes but had never smoked themselves had bought them for their parents.

(Tables 5.3-5.4)

5.4 Perceived difficulty of buying cigarettes from a shop

Smokers who usually bought their cigarettes from a shop were asked how difficult or easy they found it to do so. Almost four fifths said that, on the whole, they found it easy to purchase cigarettes from a shop. Boys were more likely than girls to say that they found it difficult (26% compared with 18%). Occasional smokers were more likely than regular smokers to say that it was difficult to buy cigarettes in a shop (32% compared with 19%), probably because occasional smokers are younger, on average, than are regular smokers.

Unsurprisingly, a higher proportion of those who were refused last time by a shopkeeper said they found it difficult to purchase cigarettes than of those who had not been refused (23% compared with 7%). Even so, 77% of those who had been refused by a shopkeeper last time still felt that, on the whole, it was easy to buy cigarettes from a shop.

(Tables 5.5- 5.6)

5.5 How many cigarettes were bought last time

The last time pupils purchased cigarettes in a shop, over half (54%) bought them in packs of ten. Although as noted above, it is illegal to sell cigarettes unpacketed, 3% of those who had bought cigarettes in a shop had bought fewer than ten. Younger pupils were more likely than older children to have bought unpackaged cigarettes: 5% of those aged 13 had done so, compared with only 2% of those aged 15, although because of the small numbers of very young smokers this difference was not statistically significant.

Occasional smokers were more likely than regular smokers to buy cigarettes in packs of ten (64% compared with 51%) whereas regular smokers were more likely to buy in packs of twenty (39% compared with 29%).

Since 1988, when the question was first asked, there has been an increase in the proportion buying packs of ten, and a corresponding decrease in the proportion buying packs of twenty: in 1988, 38% had bought a pack of ten last time, but in 1998, 54% had done so. (Tables 5.7-5.9)

5.6 How current smokers obtain their cigarettes

Current smokers were asked where they usually got their cigarettes from. If they often got cigarettes from different sources they could indicate this on the questionnaire.

During the 1990s, the usual sources of cigarettes for regular smokers have changed little, and in 1998, a similar proportion of regular smokers obtained cigarettes from each source as in 1996.

(Table 5.10)

In 1998 as in previous years most smokers bought their cigarettes from shops, with newsagents or tobacconists (65%) and garage shops (35%) being the most common retail outlets used. Sixty-one per cent of current smokers were given cigarettes by their friends while over a quarter (28%) bought them from friends and relatives: almost a quarter (24%) said that they bought cigarettes from a machine.

Younger smokers were most likely to obtain their cigarettes from friends (68% of 11/12 year-olds did so), while older smokers were most likely to buy them from newsagents or tobacconists (64% of those aged 14 and 77% of those aged 15 did so).

Regular smokers were more likely than occasional smokers to say they usually bought their cigarettes from a shop or a vending machine, whereas occasional smokers were more likely to say they were given them by friends. This difference may reflect the fact that regular smokers tend to be older than occasional smokers, and so find it easier to buy cigarettes, as well as their knowing which shops are likely to sell them cigarettes. Regular smokers were more than three times as likely as occasional smokers

to have been given cigarettes by their siblings (20% of regular smokers compared with 6% of occasional smokers)

(Tables 5.11-5.12)

All pupils were asked how often in the last year they had bought cigarettes from shops and from cigarette vending machines. Four fifths of all pupils never bought cigarettes from a shop, but 9% did so at least once a week.

The overwhelming majority of pupils (91%) said that they never bought cigarettes from a vending machine, but 4% reported that they used a vending machine at least once a month, and a further 4% did so a few times a year. Over three-quarters of those who used vending machines to purchase cigarettes said that last time they used one, it was situated in a pub, club or restaurant where alcohol was for sale.

As might be expected, older children who used vending machines were more likely to use them in places where alcohol was for sale (81% of 15 year olds compared with 65% of 11-13 year olds had done so last time). Girls were more likely than boys to buy cigarettes from vending machines in licensed premises (79% compared with 74% of those who said they used vending machines).

(Table 5.13 - 5.15)

5.7 Financing the purchase of cigarettes

Ninety-two per cent of all pupils had some money to spend each week as they liked, and the older they were, the more money they had. Eleven year olds could spend an average £4.34 a week compared with £11.62 for 15 year olds. Twenty-two per cent of 11 year olds had either no spending money or less than £1 per week, compared with only 4% of 15 year olds.

Current smokers of all ages had on average more spending money than pupils in general. Regular smokers had an average of £11.77 a week to spend as they liked, compared with occasional smokers who had an average of £9.30, and an average for all pupils of £7.83.

(Tables 5.16-5.17)

Pupils' spending money came from a number of

sources - 85% received pocket money and 25% did paid work. Not surprisingly the proportion of pupils with spending money from paid work rose with age, from 9% of 11 to 12 year olds to 43% of 15 year olds.

At each age, current smokers were more likely than non-smokers to have paid work (38% compared with 21%). They were also more likely than non-smokers to have spending money from a source other than pocket money or paid work.

(Table 5.18)

Table 5.1 Cigarette purchase in the last year, by sex :
1986 to 1998

All pupils   *England*

	Boys	Girls	Total
% who tried to buy cigarettes			
1986	25	30	27
1988	26	27	26
1990	30	33	32
1992	25	25	25
1994	24	29	26
1996	22	28	25
1998	20	23	22
Was refused at least once :			
as % of those who tried to buy them			
1986	34	28	31
1988	30	26	27
1990	40	34	37
1992	36	36	36
1994	39	32	35
1996	36	39	38
1998	44	42	43
as % of all pupils			
1986	8	9	8
1988	8	7	7
1990	12	11	12
1992	9	9	9
1994	9	9	9
1996	8	11	9
1998	8	10	9
Bases (=100%)			
Those who tried to buy cigarettes			
1986	*409*	*454*	*865*
1988	*376*	*403*	*786*
1990	*488*	*483*	*971*
1992	*412*	*399*	*811*
1994	*364*	*434*	*798*
1996	*322*	*384*	*706*
1998	*442*	*539*	*981*
All pupils			
1986	*1757*	*1495*	*3157*
1988	*1469*	*1521*	*3016*
1990	*1627*	*1465*	*3092*
1992	*1657*	*1610*	*3267*
1994	*1516*	*1517*	*3033*
1996	*1443*	*1407*	*2850*
1998	*2330*	*2411*	*4741*

Table 5.2 Cigarette purchase in the last year, by age: 1986 to 1998

All pupils   England

	11 years	12 years	13 years	14 years	15 years	Total
% who tried to buy cigarettes						
1986	16	15	21	30	45	27
1988	10	13	21	31	46	26
1990	18	18	27	39	54	32
1992	9	11	17	35	50	25
1994	7	11	19	34	55	26
1996	5	10	19	34	54	25
1998	4	6	15	32	47	22
Was refused at least once : as % of those who tried to buy them						
1986	41	47	39	30	22	31
1988	[47]	38	34	29	19	27
1990	46	52	44	31	29	36
1992	58	48	47	38	26	37
1994	[54]	42	38	42	27	35
1996	[50]	47	42	39	33	38
1998	[64]	53	51	46	36	43
as % of all pupils						
1986	7	7	8	9	10	8
1988	5	5	7	9	9	7
1990	8	9	12	12	16	12
1992	5	6	8	13	13	9
1994	4	5	7	14	15	9
1996	3	5	8	13	18	9
1998	2	3	8	14	17	9
Base (=100%)						
Those who tried to buy cigarettes						
1986	*74*	*96*	*128*	*198*	*369*	*865*
1988	*47*	*77*	*131*	*196*	*335*	*786*
1990	*105*	*110*	*158*	*234*	*360*	*971*
1992	*52*	*79*	*119*	*211*	*344*	*805*
1994	*35*	*67*	*123*	*207*	*366*	*798*
1996	*28*	*57*	*104*	*200*	*317*	*706*
1998	*22*	*42*	*102*	*401*	*661*	*982*
All pupils						
1986	*446*	*628*	*610*	*654*	*818*	*3157*
1988	*455*	*595*	*613*	*626*	*727*	*3016*
1990	*601*	*619*	*598*	*605*	*662*	*3092*
1992	*587*	*693*	*685*	*605*	*686*	*3256*
1994	*500*	*613*	*635*	*615*	*670*	*3033*
1996	*545*	*575*	*559*	*585*	*586*	*2850*
1998	*603*	*722*	*691*	*1276*	*1421*	*4742*

Table 5.3 Last time tried to buy cigarettes - who the cigarettes were for, by age

All pupils who attempted to buy cigarettes in the last year   England 1998

	11/12 years	13 years	14 years	15 years	Total	
% who were successful last time	62	71	89	94	86	
Who the cigarettes were for:						
Self	[38]	40	56	53	52	
Mother	[24]	9	5	6	7	
Father	[10]	10	2	2	4	
A friend	[27]	42	37	32	34	
Brother or sister	[4]	3	3	3	3	
Someone else	[18]	8	9	13	12	
Bases(=100%)						
All who were successful last time	*41*	*72*	*355*	*622*	*846*	
All who tried to buy in the last year	*64*	*102*	*401*	*661*	*982*	

Table 5.4 Last time tried to buy, who the cigarettes were for, by smoking behaviour

All pupils who attempted to buy cigarettes in the last year   *England 1998*

	Regular smoker	Occasional smoker	Used to smoke	Tried once	Never smoked	Total
% who were successful last time	91	83	83	85	78	86
Who the cigarettes were for :						
Self	88	37	24	3	0	52
Mother	3	2	5	14	28	7
Father	1	3	1	6	21	4
A friend	18	54	50	54	34	34
Brother or sister	2	5	4	4	4	3
Someone else	3	11	22	24	24	12
Bases(=100%)						
All who were successful last time	*393*	*144*	*121*	*98*	*86*	*842*
All who tried to buy in the last year	*433*	*174*	*145*	*115*	*110*	*977*

Table 5.5 Perceived difficulty or ease of buying cigarettes from a shop by sex, and smoking status

Smokers who had bought from shop   *England 1998*

Difficulty or ease of buying cigarettes	Sex		Smoking status		Total
	Boys	Girls	Regular smoker	Occasional smoker	
	%	%	%	%	%
Difficult	26	18	19	32	22
Easy	74	82	81	68	78
Base (=100%)	*258*	*336*	*458*	*137*	*594*

Table 5.6 Perceived difficulty or ease of buying cigarettes from a shop by whether refused by shopkeeper in the last year

Smokers who had bought from shop   *England 1998*

Difficulty or ease of buying cigarettes	Refused by shopkeeper		Total
	Yes	No	
	%	%	%
Difficult	23	7	15
Easy	77	93	85
Base (=100%)	*260*	*243*	*503*

Table 5.7 Last time cigarettes were bought - how many were bought by age

All pupils who had bought cigarettes   *England 1998*

Cigarettes bought	11/12 years	13 years	14 years	15 years	Total
	%	%	%	%	%
Fewer than 10	[4]	5	4	2	3
Ten	[51]	61	53	52	54
Twenty	[45]	31	35	40	38
More than 20	[0]	3	8	6	6
Base (=100%)	*36*	*71*	*345*	*610*	*823*

Table 5.8 Last time cigarettes were bought - how many were bought by smoking behaviour

All pupils who had bought cigarettes   *England 1998*

Cigarettes bought	Regular smoker	Occasional smoker	Used to smoke	Tried once	Never smoked	Total
	%	%	%	%	%	%
Fewer than 10	1	2	2	7	8	3
Ten	51	64	55	54	46	54
Twenty	39	29	41	35	44	38
More than 20	8	4	2	4	3	6
Base (=100%)	*388*	*140*	*119*	*97*	*77*	*821*

Table 5.9 Last time cigarettes were bought - how many were bought: 1988 to 1998

All pupils who had bought cigarettes   *England*

Cigarettes bought	1988	1990	1992	1994	1996	1998
	%	%	%	%	%	%
Fewer than 10	2	2	1	2	2	3
Ten	38	40	48	50	49	54
Twenty	54	51	45	41	44	38
More than 20	6	7	6	7	5	6
Base (=100%)	*693*	*809*	*680*	*686*	*614*	*821*

Table 5.10
Usual source of cigarettes for regular smokers: 1982 to 1998

Regular smokers   *England*

Usual source of cigarettes*	1982	1984	1986	1990	1992	1994	1996	1998
Bought from shop**	88	86	89	86	86	86	89	85
Bought from machine	13	20	19	37	27	31	32	30
Bought from friends/relatives	..	..	..	..	..	..	..	31
Bought from someone else	..	..	..	..	..	..	..	17
Bought from other people	6	12	11	18	21	23	26	..
Given by friends	44	46	39	58	62	61	55	56
Given by brother/sister	9	7	12	19	16	18	16	20
Given by mother/father	10	7	7	5	7	7	7	11
Found or taken	1	1	2	3	4	6	6	6
Other	1	3	2	8	6	11	14	11
Base (=100%)	325	474	300	305	310	348	360	496

* Percentages total more than 100 because many pupils gave more than one answer.
** Up to 1988 there was only one catergory for shop. This has been split into four since 1990, but for comparability,
in this table all the shop categories have been collapsed into one code.

Table 5.11
Usual source of cigarettes for current smokers by smoking behaviour

Current smokers   *England 1998*

Usual source of cigarettes*	Regular smokers	Occasional smokers	All current smokers
	Percentage from each source		
Bought from newsagents/ tobacconist/sweet shop	79	35	65
Bought from garage shop	44	13	35
Bought from supermarket	25	5	19
Bought from other type of shop	21	6	16
Bought from machine	30	11	24
Bought from friends/relatives	31	22	28
Bought from someone else	17	14	16
Given by friends	56	73	61
Given by brother/sister	20	6	16
Given by mother/father	11	1	8
Found or taken	6	7	7
Bases(=100%)	*496*	*232*	*727*

*Percentages total more than 100 because many pupils gave more than one answer.

Table 5.12 Usual source of cigarettes for current smokers by age

Current smokers   *England 1998*

Usual source of cigarettes*	11/12 years	13 years	14 years	15 years	All current smokers
	Percentage from each source				
Bought from newsagents/ tobacconist/sweet shop	39	49	64	77	65
Bought from garage shop	16	22	31	46	35
Bought from supermarket	6	5	16	29	19
Bought from other type of shop	10	10	13	22	16
Bought from machine	16	19	23	29	24
Bought from friends/relatives	35	39	25	25	28
Bought from someone else	21	30	12	13	16
Given by friends	68	66	64	56	61
Given by brother/sister	15	23	15	15	16
Given by mother/father	3	8	7	10	8
Found or taken	7	14	6	4	7
Bases(=100%)	*57*	*77*	*321*	*454*	*727*

*Percentages total more than 100 because many pupils gave more than one answer.

Table 5.13 How often pupils buy from shops and cigarette vending machines, by sex

All pupils   *England 1998*

	Purchase from shops			Purchase from machines		
	Boys	Girls	Total	Boys	Girls	Total
	%	%	%	%	%	%
Almost every day	4	4	4	0	0	0
Once or twice a week	4	6	5	1	1	1
Two or three times a month	2 } 12	3 } 14	2 } 13	1 } 4	1 } 4	1 } 4
About once a month	2	2	2	1	2	1
A few times a year	7	8	8	4	5	4
Never	80	78	79	92	90	91
Bases(=100%)	*2230*	*2340*	*4570*	*2143*	*2258*	*4401*

Table 5.14 Last time used cigarette vending machine - where it was situated, by age

All pupils who had used a vending machine to purchase cigarettes   *England 1998*

Where the machine was situated	11-13 years	14 years	15 years	Total
	%	%	%	%
Pub/club/restaurant- alcohol for sale	65	79	81	76
Café/restaurant - alcohol not for sale	10	2	7	6
Arcade/bowling alley	15	12	5	9
Petrol station	4	2	2	3
Holiday/abroad	6	3	4	4
Somewhere else	0	3	1	1
Bases(=100%)	*59*	*148*	*239*	*358*

Table 5.15 Last time used cigarette vending machine - where it was situated, by sex

All pupils who have used a vending machine to purchase cigarettes   *England 1998*

Where the machine was situated	Boys	Girls	Total
	%	%	%
Pub/club/restaurant- alcohol for sale	74	79	77
Café/restaurant - alcohol not for sale	6	5	6
Arcade/bowling alley	12	7	9
Petrol station	3	2	2
Holiday/abroad	3	4	4
Somewhere else	1	2	1
Bases(=100%)	*154*	*202*	*356*

Table 5.16 Amount of money pupils have to spend each week by age

All pupils

England 1998

Weekly amount	11 years	12 years	13 years	14 years	15 years	Total
	%	%	%	%	%	%
Nothing	15	10	9	5	3	8
Less than £1 a week	7	5	2	1	1	3
£1 or more but less than £5	53	46	30	20	13	32
£5 or more but less than £10	18	29	34	36	34	31
£10 or more but less than £20	4	7	18	28	30	18
£20 or more a week	4	3	6	10	18	8
Mean amount of spending money	£4.34	£5.36	£7.46	£9.74	£11.62	£7.83
Base(=100%)	572	703	684	1261	1411	4631

Table 5.17 Amount of money current smokers have to spend each week by age

Current smokers

England 1998

Weekly amount	11/12 years	13 years	14 years	15 years	Total
	%	%	%	%	%
Nothing	13	6	1	1	4
Less than £1 a week	4	4	1	2	2
£1 or more but less than £5	38	18	18	11	18
£5 or more but less than £10	31	36	35	31	33
£10 or more but less than £20	8	29	31	31	28
£20 or more a week	6	7	14	24	16
Base(=100%)	120	150	265	339	874
Mean amount of spending money					
Regular smokers	[£7.54]	£9.81	£11.41	£13.26	£11.77
Occasional smokers	£5.29	£8.80	£10.25	£11.89	£9.30
All current smokers	£5.99	£9.26	£10.95	£12.83	£10.71
All pupils	£4.90	£7.46	£9.74	£11.62	£7.83
Bases (=100%)					
Regular smokers	26	50	227	340	502
Occasional smokers	60	59	138	152	372
All current smokers	86	109	365	492	873
All pupils	1275	684	1261	1411	4615

Table 5.18 Source of money pupils have to spend each week by age and smoking behaviour

All pupils with weekly spending money

England 1998

Source *	11/12 years	13 years	14 years	15 years	Total
	%	%	%	%	%
Current smoker					
Pocket money	78	82	80	69	76
Paid work	21	27	35	50	38
Other	22	18	21	16	19
	%	%	%	%	%
Non-smoker					
Pocket money	93	89	84	76	88
Paid work	8	21	33	39	21
Other	12	14	10	11	12
	%	%	%	%	%
All pupils					
Pocket money	92	88	83	74	85
Paid work	9	22	34	43	25
Other	13	14	14	13	13
Base(=100%)					
Current smokers	76	104	364	487	838
Non-smokers	1047	520	846	882	3338
All pupils with spending money	1123	624	1210	1369	4176

* Percentages total more than 100 because some pupils could have more than one source.

6 Drinking - Introduction

6.1 **Background**

Although the 1998 survey is the latest in a biennial series which began in 1982, drinking was not covered until 1988, when only a very few general questions were included. In 1990, the section was expanded to provide estimates of consumption of different types of drink, and in 1996, it was modified further to include alcopops (alcoholic lemonades and similar drinks), and to collect a little more information about the circumstances in which 11-15 year olds drink. The only substantive change made in 1998 was the addition of a question asking those who had had an alcoholic drink in the last week, the days of the week on which they had done so.

6.2 **Measuring self-reported alcohol consumption**

In recent years, the range of alcoholic drinks available has grown but practical constraints make it impossible to ask about every type of drink individually. Pupils who had drunk alcohol in the last seven days were asked how much they had drunk of each of the following six types of drink:

● beer, lager and cider;
● shandy;
● wine;
● martini and sherry;
● spirits and liqueurs
● alcoholic lemonade, alcoholic cola or other alcoholic soft drinks.

The last category listed above was included for the first time in 1996.

Answers could be given in terms of pints, half pints, large cans, small cans and bottles for beer, lager, cider and shandy, in glasses for wine,

fortified wine and spirits, and in bottles or cans for alcopops. Pupils could also indicate if they had drunk less than one of the standard measures, and they were asked not to count low alcohol drinks.

It might be thought that children of this age would tend to be untruthful about their drinking. There is no evidence on this point relating specifically to drinking, but, as discussed in Chapter 2, this series of surveys does have biochemical evidence in relation to self-reported smoking among this age group: it has been shown consistently that in each survey, only a handful of children out of several thousand say they don't smoke when they do. It seems reasonable, therefore, to assume that they are also unlikely to deny the fact that they do drink, but there is still uncertainty about the accuracy of reported levels of consumption. Four boys have been excluded from the analysis of last week's alcohol consumption - they reported totals of 174, 132, 67 and 55 units in the last week, and inspection of their answers to individual questions suggested either that they were not taking the survey seriously or that they had misunderstood the questions. There were a further 11 pupils who had drunk more than 50 units in the week: their answers were also inspected, and in each case the pattern of answers to individual questions was consistent and believable, so there was no reason to exclude them from the analysis.

Under-reporting of consumption is a more serious problem than overstatement. All surveys are known to underestimate how much people drink - for a variety of reasons, but mainly because they forget. Another important factor is that on most surveys, all beers, lagers and ciders are assumed to be of the same alcoholic strength: it is usually impractical to collect sufficient information about what people drink to be able to assess this accurately. The 1989 survey of adult drinking carried out by OPCS[1] was able to look at this in detail, and found that if variation in alcoholic strength was taken into account, consumption of those aged 16-24 increased by about one fifth for young men and one tenth for young women. Although that age group drinks more than those aged 11-15, the types of drink drunk are probably similar, and the alcohol consumption of those covered by this survey is likely to be underestimated for the same reason.

References

1   Goddard E, *Drinking in England & Wales in the late 1980s,* 1991 (London HMSO)

7 Drinking in the previous week

7.1 Drinking frequency

In 1998, 21% of children aged 11-15 in England said that they had had an alcoholic drink in the last seven days, a statistically significant decrease compared with 1996, when 27% had done so. The decrease was significant for both boys and girls, but somewhat more marked among girls. Thus in 1998, 23% of boys, compared with 18% of girls, had had a drink in the last week. This difference between boys and girls contrasts with the results for 1996, which showed boys and girls equally likely to have had a drink last week, but is similar to the pattern established in earlier years of the survey.

These latest figures make it difficult to interpret trends since 1988, when the series of surveys started collecting information about drinking in England. Before the data for 1998 were added to the series, it appeared that although there had been no clear rise in the proportion of children of this age who drink at all, there had been a fairly marked increase in the frequency with which those who drank did so: the proportion of pupils aged 11-15 who had had an drink in the previous week rose from 20% in 1988 to 27% in 1996. It is not possible to tell whether the decrease in 1998 is the start of a new trend, or whether, with hindsight, the results for 1998 will seem a little out of line.

As in previous surveys, the proportions drinking last week increased sharply with age, as would be expected: only 3% of 11 year olds had done so, compared with 44% of 15 year olds. On the whole the decrease between 1996 and 1998 occurred throughout the age range.

(Figure 7.1, Tables 7.1-7.2)

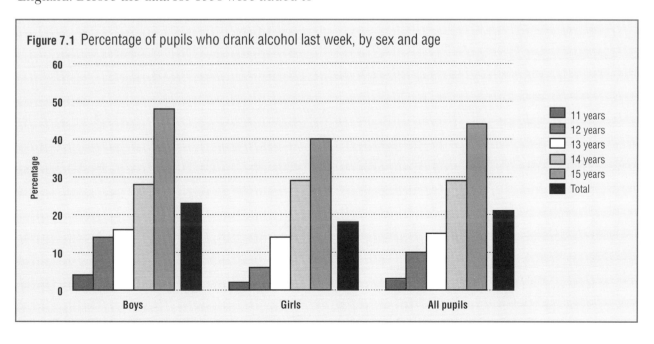

Figure 7.1 Percentage of pupils who drank alcohol last week, by sex and age

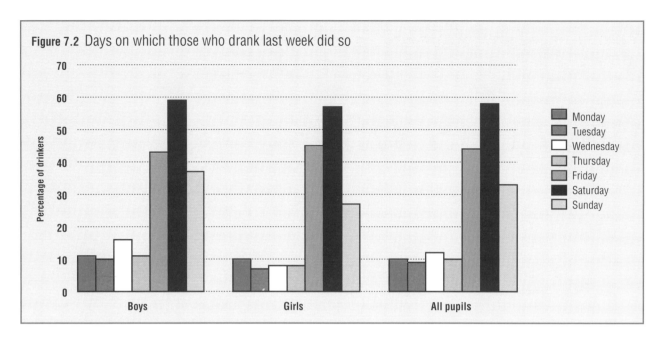

Figure 7.2 Days on which those who drank last week did so

7.2 Drinking days in the last week

In 1998, drinkers were asked for the first time on which days in the last week they had had an alcoholic drink.

Four in five of those who had a drink in the last week had done so on only one or two days, but a small proportion, 4%, said they had done so on five or more days. Boys were much more likely than girls to have had a drink on several days - 6% of boy drinkers compared with 2% of girl drinkers had drunk alcohol on five or more days in the week.

Weekends were the most popular time for a drink: 58% of those who had had an alcoholic drink in the last week had had a drink on the Saturday, 44% on the Friday, and 33% on the Sunday.

(Figure 7.2, Tables 7.3-7.4)

7.3 Alcohol consumption

It should be noted that the results which follow are based on the alcohol consumption of those who drank alcohol in the week before interview – that is, just 21% of all 11-15 year olds. The behaviour of this group should not be taken to be representative of all 11-15 year olds who drink. This is because less frequent drinkers are younger, on average, and may, for example, prefer different types of drink, and drink different amounts when they do drink. The

information given is, however, representative of what this age group drinks in a typical week, so some tables in this section give averages based on all pupils, as well as on those who drank in the previous week.

7.4 Average weekly alcohol consumption per pupil

The average weekly amount drunk per pupil aged 11-15 in 1998 was 1.6 units (somewhat less than a pint of beer, or its equivalent). Boys continue to drink more, on average, than do girls – in 1998, boys had drunk an average of 1.9 units in the previous seven days, compared with an average of 1.2 units for girls. These average amounts conceal wide variation in the amounts children of this age drink. The overwhelming majority had drunk little or nothing in the previous seven days, and most of the remainder had drunk only modest amounts. However, at the other end of the scale, 4% of boys and 2% of girls had drunk 15 or more units in the previous week.

The average weekly alcohol consumption of 1.6 units in 1998 was less than the estimate of 1.8 in 1996, but still double the figure of 0.8 units in 1990: the fall in 1998 followed a fairly steady increase between 1990 and 1996, and one which occurred to a similar degree among both boys and girls.

(Figures 7.3-7.4, Tables 7.5-7.10)

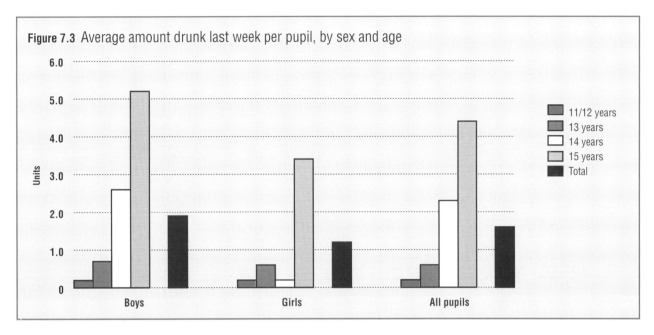

Figure 7.3 Average amount drunk last week per pupil, by sex and age

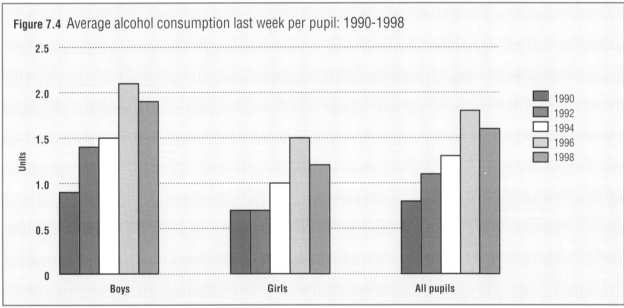

Figure 7.4 Average alcohol consumption last week per pupil: 1990-1998

7.5 **Average weekly alcohol consumption per drinker**

The slight decrease in the average weekly amount drunk noted above is due almost entirely to the fall in the proportion of pupils who had had a drink in the previous week. This is illustrated by Table 7.7, which shows trends in the average amount drunk by those who had drunk alcohol in the last seven days (ie those who had not drunk in the last week are excluded from the averages). Far from falling in 1998, the average amount drunk last week by those who did drink increased again, from 8.4 units in 1996 to 9.9 units. Thus, although the proportion drinking in the previous week had fallen in 1998 compared with 1996, those who did drink, drank more.

Consumption per drinker was higher for boys than for girls - boys had drunk on average 11.3 units in the previous week, compared with 8.4 units for girls, and a much higher proportion (25% compared with 15%) had drunk 15 units or more. These differences in alcohol consumption between boys and girls are consistent with differences established in surveys of adult drinking - young men aged 16-17 drink considerably more than young women of the same age.

Among drinkers aged 15, the average amount drunk in the previous week was 12.9 units for boys - the same as in 1996. For girls, however, it was 9.7 units, still lower than for boys of the same age, but a marked increase compared with 8.0

units in 1996. Indeed, in 1996, as many as one fifth of girls aged 15 who had drunk alcohol last week (one in twelve of all girls aged 15) had drunk 15 or more units in the week. The equivalent figure for boys nevertheless continued to be much higher, at 30% of drinkers and one in seven of all boys aged 15, even though the amount they drank did not rise in 1998.

(Tables 7.7-7.10)

7.6 **Types of drink**

As noted earlier, the 1998 survey repeated questions included for the first time in 1996 about alcopops - alcoholic lemonades, colas, and other alcoholic soft drinks. These are sweet tasting drinks with a relatively high alcoholic content of up to about 5% - similar in strength to many lagers and ciders. The first brand was launched in the summer of 1995.

In 1998, 14% of all 11-15 year olds - 16% of boys and 11% of girls - had drunk beer, lager or cider in the last week; 10% had drunk wine, and the same proportion had drunk spirits. Only 7% had drunk alcopops and even smaller proportions had drunk shandy and fortified wine. Between 1990 and 1996, the proportion of pupils drinking shandy, wine, and fortified wine stayed much the same, but the proportions drinking beer lager and cider and spirits rose. In 1998, however, the proportion drinking beer, lager and cider fell to 14% from 19% in 1996. There was also a marked fall in the proportion drinking alcopops, which halved from 14% in 1996 to 7% in 1998.

Almost three quarters of those who had drunk alcohol in the week before interview had drunk beer, lager or cider at some time during the week. The type of drink mentioned next most frequently was spirits (54%), and wine (51%) followed by alcopops (37%), and then fortified wine (20%). (The percentages do not, of course, add up to 100%, because many pupils had drunk more than one type of drink during the week.) Boys were more likely than girls to have drunk beer, lager and cider, and less likely than girls to have drunk each of the other types of drink except shandy. It should be noted that these differences are based on a relatively small number of drinkers, and the difference in the proportions drinking spirits is not statistically significant.

Since older pupils were much more likely to have had a drink last week than were younger children, the proportion of pupils who had drunk each type of drink in the last week also increased with age. However, analysis restricted to those who drank last week throws some light on the relative popularity of different drinks for each age group. Beer lager and cider was the most common type of drink overall, and more than 70% of drinkers aged 13, 14 and 15 had drunk these types of drink in the last week. However, for the first time in this series of surveys, wine appeared to be at least as popular as beer lager and cider among the youngest drinkers: 60% of 11 and 12 year old drinkers had drunk beer lager and cider in the last week, and 69% had drunk wine (the difference is not statistically significant so it is not possible to say that wine has become *more* popular).

In 1998, for the first time, those who had drunk beer, lager or cider in the previous week were asked whether they usually drank normal strength or strong beers, and 27% said they usually drank strong beers rather than normal strength ones. However, 17% were unable to give an answer. The proportion not answering varied markedly according to how much of these types of drink they had drunk in the last week. More than one half of those who had drunk less than 2 units of beer lager or cider in the last week were unable to answer, probably because they did not drink beer lager or cider regularly enough to know what strength their drinks were.

Those who drank the most beer, lager and cider were the most likely to drink strong brands: 42% of those who had drunk 10 or more units of beer lager and cider in the last week said they drank the strong type.

The report on the 1996 survey discussed in some detail effect on young drinkers of the introduction of alcopops. It concluded that alcopops were probably mainly an additional drink option for children who would have been drinking anyway, although the data provided some support for the suggestion that those who drink alcopops may do so because the taste of alcohol is masked by the addition of fruit juice or cola.

The data for 1998 reflect the speed with which fashions in drinking can change among this age group: in 1996, a year or so after they were introduced into the market, they were the second most popular drink among this age group, but two years later they had fallen well behind spirits and wine.

(Tables 7.11-7.14)

7.7 **Alcohol consumption of different types of drink**

Beers were much more likely to have been drunk in large quantities in the last seven days than were other types of drink, but even so, amounts were moderate for most drinkers: one quarter of those who had drunk beer, lager or cider in the last week had drunk less than a pint in total during the week. The amounts reported for other types of alcohol were even lower - for example, 57% of shandy drinkers had drunk less than a pint, one third of those who had drunk spirits said they had drunk less than a single measure, and a similar proportion of those who had drunk alcopops had drunk less than one bottle or can. However, 14% of those who had drunk beer lager or cider (2% of all pupils aged 11-15) had drunk 15 units or more during the previous week: this is more than a pint a day, on average.

(Figure 7.5, Tables 7.15-7.16)

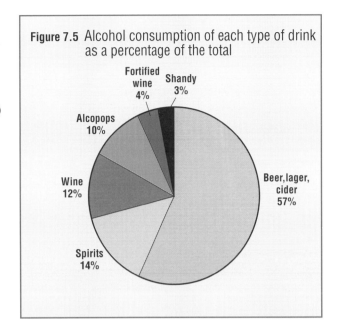

Figure 7.5 Alcohol consumption of each type of drink as a percentage of the total

Fortified wine 4%
Shandy 3%
Alcopops 10%
Wine 12%
Spirits 14%
Beer, lager, cider 57%

Table 7.1 When last had a drink, by sex: 1988 to 1998

All pupils   *England*

When last had a drink	1988	1990	1992	1994	1996	1998
	%	%	%	%	%	%
Boys						
During the last week	24	22	24	26	27	23
One to four weeks ago	19	15	12	14	15	15
One to six months ago	12	13	13	11	12	12
More than six months ago	11	15	14	10	9	12
Never had a drink	35	35	37	39	37	38
Base (=100%)	*1427*	*1619*	*1646*	*1503*	*1432*	*2249*
	%	%	%	%	%	%
Girls						
During the last week	17	20	17	22	26	18
One to four weeks ago	17	14	12	16	13	15
One to six months ago	13	13	14	12	13	13
More than six months ago	11	15	12	10	10	11
Never had a drink	41	38	44	40	38	42
Base (=100%)	*1518*	*1456*	*1606*	*1506*	*1391*	*2362*
	%	%	%	%	%	%
Total						
During the last week	20	21	21	24	27	21
One to four weeks ago	18	15	12	15	14	15
One to six months ago	12	13	13	11	12	13
More than six months ago	11	15	13	10	9	11
Never had a drink	38	36	41	39	38	40
Base (=100%)	*3015*	*3082*	*3252*	*3009*	*2823*	*4609*

Table 7.2 Percentage who drank last week, by sex and age: 1988 to 1998

All pupils   *England*

Sex and age	1988	1990	1992	1994	1996	1998	*1998 base (=100%)**
				Percentage who drank last week			
Boys							
11 years	7	8	8	8	7	4	*285*
12 years	12	9	13	10	12	14	*336*
13 years	20	17	15	22	27	16	*293*
14 years	25	32	32	34	37	28	*597*
15 years	45	42	49	52	50	48	*745*
Total	24	22	24	26	27	23	*2256*
Girls							
11 years	4	4	5	4	6	2	*291*
12 years	7	6	7	9	9	6	*365*
13 years	11	19	11	16	22	14	*383*
14 years	19	32	25	26	35	29	*657*
15 years	36	39	40	48	55	40	*666*
Total	17	20	17	22	26	18	*2362*
All pupils							
11 years	5	6	6	6	7	3	*577*
12 years	9	8	10	9	11	10	*702*
13 years	16	18	13	19	24	15	*675*
14 years	22	32	29	30	36	29	*1254*
15 years	40	40	45	50	53	44	*1409*
Total	20	21	21	24	27	21	*4617*

* Bases for previous years are shown in earlier reports

Table 7.3 Number of drinking days in the last week, by age and sex

Those who drank last week   *England 1998*

Number of drinking days	11/12 years	13 years	14 years	15 years	Total
Boys					
1	69	[62]	60	50	57
2	20	[22]	19	23	21
3	5	[5]	11	13	10
4	0	[8]	6	8	6
5	2	[0]	2	2	2
6	0	[0]	1	1	1
7	5	[3]	2	3	3
Average	1.6	[1.7]	1.8	2.0	1.9
Base (=100%)	*61*	*46*	*176*	*358*	*528*
Girls					
1	[88]	80	60	55	64
2	[7]	3	23	26	20
3	[5]	3	12	14	10
4	[0]	12	3	3	4
5	[0]	0	0	1	0
6	[0]	0	1	1	1
7	[0]	3	0	0	1
Average	1.2	1.6	1.6	1.7	1.6
Base (=100%)	*32*	*53*	*206*	*269*	*444*
Total					
1	75	72	60	52	60
2	16	12	22	24	21
3	4	4	12	13	10
4	0	10	4	6	5
5	2	0	1	1	1
6	0	0	1	1	1
7	3	2	1	2	2
Average	1.5	1.6	1.7	1.9	1.8
Base (=100%)	*92*	*99*	*382*	*625*	*968*

Table 7.4 Days on which children drank last week, by age and sex

Those who drank last week   *England 1998*

Drinking days	11/12 years	13 years	14 years	15 years	Total
Boys					
Sunday	39	[42]	32	37	37
Monday	14	[11]	9	11	11
Tuesday	17	[5]	10	10	10
Wednesday	16	[17]	16	16	16
Thursday	6	[19]	7	12	11
Friday	18	[27]	47	54	43
Saturday	54	[52]	57	63	59
Base (=100%)	*61*	*46*	*175*	*357*	*526*
Girls					
Sunday	[38]	22	28	27	27
Monday	[17]	15	9	7	10
Tuesday	[4]	9	6	8	7
Wednesday	[0]	10	9	8	8
Thursday	[5]	13	7	7	8
Friday	[24]	34	45	53	45
Saturday	[29]	57	58	62	57
Base (=100%)	*31*	*53*	*206*	*269*	*442*
Total					
Sunday	39	31	30	33	33
Monday	15	13	9	9	10
Tuesday	12	7	8	9	9
Wednesday	11	13	12	13	12
Thursday	6	16	7	10	10
Friday	20	31	46	54	44
Saturday	45	54	58	63	58
Base (=100%)	*93*	*99*	*381*	*626*	*969*

Table 7.5 Alcohol consumption in the last seven days, by sex: 1990 to 1998

All pupils   *England*

Alcohol consumption (units)	1990	1992	1994	1996	1998
	%	%	%	%	%
Boys					
None	84	80	79	78	83
Less than 1.00	2	2	3	1	1
1.00-1.75	2	3	3	3	2
2.00-3.73	3	4	3	4	3
4.00-5.75	2	2	3	2	2
6.00-9.75	2	4	4	5	3
10.00-14.75	2	2	2	2	3
15.00 or more	2	2	3	5	4
Mean	0.9	1.4	1.5	2.1	1.9
Base (=100%)	*1499*	*1581*	*1429*	*1346*	*2093*
	%	%	%	%	%
Girls					
None	86	86	81	78	85
Less than 1.00	2	3	2	2	1
1.00-1.75	2	2	4	3	2
2.00-3.73	3	3	5	5	3
4.00-5.75	2	2	2	4	2
6.00-9.75	3	3	3	3	3
10.00-14.75	1	1	2	2	2
15.00 or more	1	1	1	3	2
Mean	0.7	0.7	1.0	1.5	1.2
Base (=100%)	*1358*	*1561*	*1460*	*1330*	*2273*
	%	%	%	%	%
Total					
None	86	83	80	78	84
Less than 1.00	2	2	2	2	1
1.00-1.75	2	2	3	3	2
2.00-3.73	3	4	4	5	3
4.00-5.75	2	2	2	3	2
6.00-9.75	2	4	4	4	3
10.00-14.75	2	1	2	2	2
15.00 or more	1	2	2	4	3
Mean	0.8	1.1	1.3	1.8	1.6
Base (=100%)	*2857*	*3142*	*2889*	*2676*	*4367*

Table 7.6 Mean alcohol consumption in the last seven days, by sex and age: 1990 to 1998

All pupils   *England*

Sex and age	1990	1992	1994	1996	1998	*1998 base**
			Mean number of units			
Boys						
11/12 years	0.1	0.2	0.2	0.2	0.2	*597*
13 years	0.6	0.4	0.8	1.7	0.7	*277*
14 years	1.2	1.5	1.9	2.2	2.6	*553*
15 years	2.5	4.4	4.2	6.0	5.2	*660*
Total	0.9	1.4	1.5	2.1	1.9	*2086*
Girls						
11/12 years	0.1	0.1	0.1	0.1	0.2	*651*
13 years	0.3	0.4	0.5	1.0	0.6	*366*
14 years	1.3	0.8	1.2	2.5	2.0	*621*
15 years	1.7	2.2	2.8	4.0	3.4	*625*
Total	0.7	0.7	1.0	1.5	1.2	*2262*
All pupils						
11/12 years	0.1	0.2	0.2	0.2	0.2	*1248*
13 years	0.4	0.4	0.6	1.3	0.6	*642*
14 years	1.2	1.1	1.6	2.4	2.3	*1174*
15 years	2.1	3.4	3.5	5.0	4.4	*1284*
Total	0.8	1.1	1.3	1.8	1.6	*4347*

* Bases for previous years are shown in earlier reports

Table 7.7 Mean alcohol consumption of those who had drunk in the last seven days, by sex: 1990 to 1998

Those who had drunk in the last seven days   *England*

Sex and age	1990	1992	1994	1996	1998	1998 base*
						Mean number of units
Boys						
11-13 years	..	3.6	5.2	7.1	6.2	55
14 years	..	5.3	6.7	7.3	12.3	122
15 years	..	9.6	8.8	12.9	12.9	266
Total	5.7	7.0	7.4	9.7	11.3	351
Girls						
11-13 years	..	3.1	3.0	4.0	6.4	53
14 years	..	3.8	5.5	8.2	8.1	160
15 years	..	6.0	6.6	8.0	9.7	221
Total	4.7	4.7	5.4	7.0	8.4	334
All pupils						
11-13 years	..	3.4	4.1	5.5	6.3	108
14 years	..	4.7	6.1	7.7	9.9	282
15 years	..	8.1	7.7	10.4	11.5	487
Total	5.3	6.0	6.4	8.4	9.9	686

* Bases for previous years are shown in earlier reports

Table 7.8 Alcohol consumption in the last seven days, by sex
   (a) all pupils
   (b) those who had drunk in the last seven days

England 1998

Alcohol consumption (units)	(a) all pupils			(b) those who had drunk in the last seven days		
	Boys	Girls	Total	Boys	Girls	Total
	%	%	%	%	%	%
None	83	85	84	..	..	..
Less than 1.00	1	1	1	4	6	5
1.00-1.75	2	2	2	10	12	12
2.00-3.73	3	3	3	17	20	18
4.00-5.75	2	2	2	12	13	12
6.00-9.75	3	3	3	16	18	17
10.00-14.75	3	2	2	16	15	16
15.00 or more	4	2	3	25	15	20
Mean number of units	1.9	1.2	1.6	11.3	8.4	9.9
Base (=100%)	*2093*	*2273*	*4367*	*349*	*336*	*687*

Table 7.9 Mean alcohol consumption in the last seven days, by sex and age
   (a) all pupils
   (b) those who had drunk in the last seven days

England 1998

Age	(a) all pupils			(b) those who had drunk in the last seven days		
	Boys	Girls	Total	Boys	Girls	Total
	Mean number of units			*Mean number of units*		
11-13 years	0.4	0.3	0.4	6.2	6.4	6.3
14 years	2.6	2.0	2.3	12.3	8.1	9.9
15 years	5.2	3.4	4.4	12.9	9.7	11.5
Total	1.9	1.2	1.6	11.3	8.4	9.9
Base (=100%)						
11-13 years	*873*	*1017*	*1890*	*55*	*53*	*108*
14 years	*553*	*621*	*1174*	*122*	*160*	*282*
15 years	*660*	*625*	*1284*	*266*	*221*	*487*
Total	*2086*	*2262*	*4347*	*351*	*334*	*686*

Table 7.10 Alcohol consumption of 15 year olds in the last seven days, by sex
(a) all pupils aged 15
(b) those aged 15 who had drunk in the last seven days

Pupils aged 15   *England 1998*

Alcohol consumption (units)	(a) all pupils			(b) those who had drunk in the last seven days		
	Boys	Girls	Total	Boys	Girls	Total
	%	%	%	%	%	%
None	60	65	62	..	..	..
Less than 1.00	1	1	1	3	3	3
1.00-1.75	3	3	3	6	7	7
2.00-3.73	6	6	6	14	18	16
4.00-5.75	5	5	5	12	14	13
6.00-9.75	6	8	6	14	21	17
10.00-14.75	8	5	7	20	15	18
15.00 or more	12	7	10	30	21	26
Mean	5.2	3.4	4.4	12.9	9.7	11.5
Base (=100%)	*660*	*625*	*1284*	*266*	*221*	*487*

Table 7.11 Types of alcohol drunk in the last seven days, by sex: 1990 to 1998
(a) percentage of all pupils
(b) percentage of those who had drunk in the last seven days

England

	1990	1992	1994	1996	1998	1990	1992	1994	1996	1998
	(a) % of all pupils					(b) % of those who had drunk in the last seven days				
	%	%	%	%	%	%	%	%	%	%
Boys										
Beer, lager, cider	16	20	21	21	16	76	81	82	81	78
Shandy	8	6	7	6	4	38	26	27	22	19
Wine	9	11	11	10	10	44	46	44	38	47
Fortified wine	3	4	3	3	3	14	15	12	11	16
Spirits	7	9	9	11	11	33	38	37	42	52
Alcopops	..	..	..	14	7	..	..	..	52	33
Base (=100%)	*1610*	*1648*	*1497*	*1421*	*2226*	*339*	*394*	*375*	*372*	*446*
	%	%	%	%	%	%	%	%	%	%
Girls										
Beer, lager, cider	11	12	15	17	11	56	67	70	67	63
Shandy	4	4	5	5	3	22	23	21	18	18
Wine	11	10	11	11	10	56	60	52	43	55
Fortified wine	4	3	4	5	4	22	20	18	19	24
Spirits	7	6	9	12	10	38	36	42	48	56
Alcopops	..	..	..	15	7	..	..	..	58	42
Base (=100%)	*1445*	*1612*	*1508*	*1380*	*2367*	*284*	*275*	*324*	*349*	*410*
	%	%	%	%	%	%	%	%	%	%
Total										
Beer, lager, cider	14	16	18	19	14	67	76	76	74	71
Shandy	6	5	6	5	4	31	25	24	20	18
Wine	10	11	11	10	10	50	52	48	40	51
Fortified wine	4	4	3	4	4	18	17	15	15	20
Spirits	7	8	9	12	10	35	37	39	45	54
Alcopops	..	..	..	14	7	..	..	..	55	37
Base (=100%)	*3055*	*3260*	*3005*	*2801*	*4593*	*623*	*669*	*699*	*721*	*856*

Table 7.12 Types of alcohol drunk in the last seven days, by age:
 (a) percentage of those who had drunk in the last seven days who had drunk each type of drink
 (b) percentage of all pupils who had drunk each typeof drink

England 1998

Type of drink	11 years	12 years	13 years	14 years	15 years	Total
(a) % of all pupils						
Beer, lager, cider	1	5	9	19	31	14
Shandy	1	2	4	4	5	4
Wine	2	6	7	15	18	10
Fortified wine	0	2	2	6	8	4
Spirits	1	4	5	16	24	10
Alcopops	1	3	5	12	14	7
Base (=100%)	*578*	*705*	*676*	*1255*	*1389*	*4603*
(a) % of those who had drunk in the last seven days						
Beer, lager, cider		60	72	71	74	71
Shandy		30	32	17	13	18
Wine		69	52	55	44	51
Fortified wine		17	20	24	18	20
Spirits		49	38	57	58	54
Alcopops		32	36	44	34	37
Base (=100%)		*68*	*86*	*352*	*569*	*855*

Table 7.13 Whether usually drinks strong or normal strength beers by sex and age

Those who drank beer lager or cider last week   *England 1998*

Type of beer, lager, cider	11-13 years	14 years	15 years	Total
Boys	%	%	%	%
Can't say	27	9	10	14
Normal strength	48	53	62	56
Strong	25	38	28	30
Base (=100%)	*59*	*126*	*277*	*368*
Girls	%	%	%	%
Can't say	43	15	14	21
Normal strength	41	63	59	56
Strong	16	22	26	22
Base (=100%)	*46*	*126*	*156*	*258*
Total	%	%	%	%
Can't say	34	11	12	17
Normal strength	45	58	61	56
Strong	21	30	28	27
Base (=100%)	*105*	*252*	*432*	*625*

Table 7.14 Whether usually drinks strong or normal strength beers by sex and amount drunk last week

Those who drank beer lager or cider last week   *England 1998*

Type of beer, lager, cider	Amount of beer, lager cider drunk last week				Total
	Less than 2 units	2.00-5.75 units	6.00-9.75 units	10 units or more	
Boys	%	%	%	%	%
Can't say	54	3	3	4	14
Normal strength	38	70	62	51	56
Strong	8	28	35	45	30
Base (=100%)	*74*	*112*	*69*	*109*	*364*
Girls	%	%	%	%	%
Can't say	60	1	2	10	21
Normal strength	30	74	66	56	56
Strong	10	24	33	33	23
Base (=100%)	*82*	*82*	*55*	*39*	*258*
Total	%	%	%	%	%
Can't say	57	2	2	6	17
Normal strength	35	72	65	52	56
Strong	8	26	34	42	27
Base (=100%)	*156*	*194*	*122*	*148*	*620*

Table 7.15 Alcohol consumption of different types of drink by those who had drunk in the last seven days
(a) percentage of all who had drunk in the last seven days
(b) percentage of those who had drunk that type of drink

England 1998

Alcohol consumption (units)	Beer, lager cider	Shandy	Wine	Martini, sherry	Spirits	Alcopops
(a) percentage of all who had drunk in the last seven days						
None	20	82	51	82	48	64
Less than 1.00	16	10	14	7	16	11
1.00-1.75	3	3	8	4	7	5
2.00-3.73	15	3	16	5	14	10
4.00-5.75	10	1	6	2	9	7
6.00-9.75	16	1	3	1	4	3
10.00-14.75	9	0	1	0	2	1
15.00 or more	11	0	0	0	0	0
Mean number of units	5.7	0.3	1.2	0.4	1.4	1.0
Base (=100%)	690	687	687	689	683	687
(b) percentage of those who had drunk that type of drink						
Less than 1.00	22	57	31	41	33	32
1.00-1.75	4	14	16	20	12	13
2.00-3.73	18	18	32	25	27	26
4.00-5.75	13	5	12	9	16	17
6.00-9.75	20	4	6	3	8	8
10.00-14.75	10	1	3	1	3	4
15.00 or more	14	1	0	1	1	1
Mean number of units	7.1	1.5	2.3	1.9	2.7	2.9
Base (=100%)	621	156	434	167	458	317

Table 7.16 Alcohol consumption (units) of different types of drink: 1992 to 1998

Those who had drunk in the last seven days *England*

Type of drink	1992	1994	1996	1998
Mean number of units				
Beer, lager, cider	3.7	4.0	4.7	5.7
Shandy	0.2	0.2	0.2	0.3
Wine	1.0	0.9	0.7	1.2
Fortified wine	0.3	0.2	0.2	0.4
Spirits	0.8	1.0	1.2	1.4
Alcopops	..	..	1.4	1.0
Total	6.0	6.4	8.4	9.9
Base	544	569	585	686

8 Usual drinking behaviour

8.1 Introduction

All those who said they drank alcohol, even if they had not done so in the previous week, were asked a few questions about their drinking - how often they usually had a drink, where they drank, who they were usually with, and if they bought alcohol, where they usually bought it. It should be borne in mind when considering the results that follow that asking about usual drinking behaviour is not ideal, because many children of this age do not have settled regular patterns of behaviour, and some may have found the questions difficult to answer (this difficulty was noted in the previous chapter in relation to whether they drank strong or normal strength beers). The alternative would have been to ask about the last time they had a drink, but this approach was rejected: general conclusions about the drinking behaviour of this age group cannot be drawn directly from such questions, because they do not take account of the fact that some children drink much more frequently than others.

8.2 Usual drinking frequency

The first question in the section on drinking asks pupils if they have 'ever had a proper alcoholic drink - a whole drink, not just a sip'. The intention of starting with this question is to avoid asking the detailed questions that follow of those who have had only small amounts of alcohol - perhaps a sip of a parent's drink on special occasions. It has been suggested that some children who share drinks with their friends may also answer no at this question. Although this is

in theory possible, it is unlikely that they would never have had a whole drink, and there is no evidence from the questionnaires or feedback from the interviewers to support this suggestion.

Two fifths of the sample said that they had never had a proper alcoholic drink, and a further 4% said that they had done so, but did not drink at all now. Table 8.1 also shows clearly how the frequency with which children drink increases with age - 74% of 11 year olds said they had never had a proper drink, compared with only 12% of 15 year olds. As noted in the previous chapter, the drinking behaviour of most children aged 11-15 is relatively modest: even among the oldest pupils, most drank no more than once a week. However, a small but significant proportion of those aged 15, 4% of boys and 2% of girls, said that they drank almost every day.

These data on usual drinking frequency are consistent with the proportions who said that they had had a drink in the previous week. Table 8.1 shows that 16% said they usually drank at least weekly. To these may be added half of the 7% who said they drank once a fortnight, and one quarter of the 9% who said they drank monthly, giving a total of about 22% who might be found drinking in a typical week. This compares well with the 21% who said they did drink in the previous week (see Table 7.1).

The proportion of children who said that they usually drank at least once a week fell from 20% in 1996 to 16% in 1998. This is consistent with the decrease noted earlier in the proportion who actually had a drink in the last week, except that the latter was more marked among girls than among boys, whereas the change in usual behaviour was similar for boys and girls.

(Tables 8.1-8.2)

8.3 Usual circumstances in which children drink

Pupils were asked where they usually drank, and, reflecting their varied behaviour, many gave more than one answer. The place of drinking mentioned by the highest proportion of drinkers was their own home or the home of a relative or friend - 58% said this was where they usually drank, compared with 23% saying they drank at parties, 12% saying they usually drank in pubs, and 10% in clubs or discos[1]. In addition, 21% of drinkers said they usually drank at places other than those mentioned: this answer would probably have been given mainly by those who drink out in the open - for example in the street or in the park.

The proportion who said they drank at home fell from 79% among 11 year old drinkers to 51% among drinkers aged 15. Even among 15 year olds, however, among whom there was a much higher proportion who drank at parties and in pubs and clubs, someone's home was the place mentioned most often. Reflecting their greater opportunities for drinking and their wider experience of doing so, older drinkers were much more likely than younger drinkers to mention more than one place as somewhere they often drank. In 1996, girls were more likely than

boys to say they drank in pubs and clubs, but in 1998 there were no significant differences between boys and girls.

In the same way as where children drink varies as they get older, so does who they drink with. Seven in ten of the youngest drinkers said they were usually with their parents when they had an alcoholic drink. At the other end of the age range, although as many as three in ten 15 year olds still drank with their parents, many more said they were usually with friends when they had a drink.

At all ages except the youngest, girls were more likely than boys to drink with a mixed-sex group of friends. At age 15, girls were relatively more likely to have a drink with their boyfriends, whereas boys were more likely to drink with other boys.

Because older children drink more often than younger children, it is possible that the association described above between drinking circumstances and age may be more due to drinking frequency than age. Tables 8.5 and 8.6 show how drinking circumstances vary according to age and whether the pupil usually drank at least once a week or less often than that. In fact, who they usually drink with, and to some extent, who they are with, appear to be related to both age and drinking frequency. So, for example, at each age, frequent drinkers were more likely to drink with a mixed sex group of friends at each age than were infrequent drinkers, and for both groups, the proportion doing so increased with age.

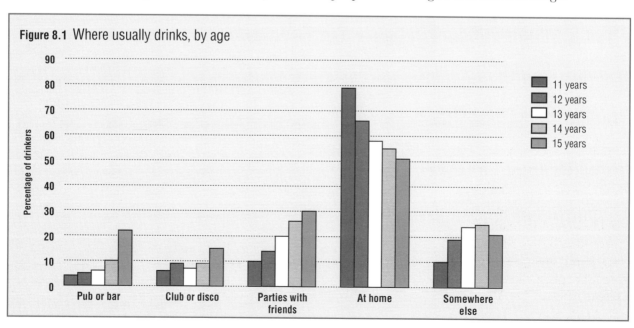

Figure 8.1 Where usually drinks, by age

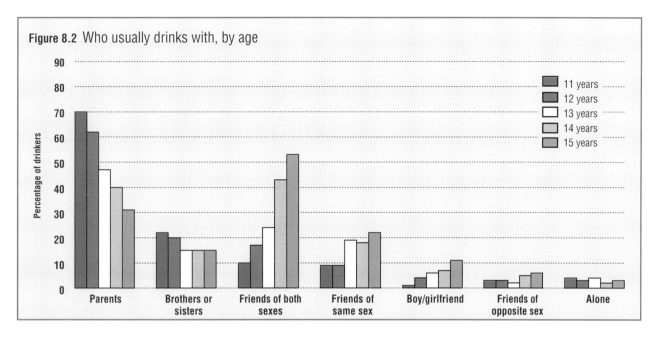

Figure 8.2 Who usually drinks with, by age

There appears to have been a fall in the proportion of girl drinkers who say they usually drink on licensed premises, so that in 1998 girls were no more likely than boys to say these were places where they usually drank. The other significant change between 1996 and 1998 was an increase in the proportion saying they usually drank at home or in someone else's home, and a corresponding fall in the proportion saying 'somewhere else' which is likely to be predominantly drinking out of doors.

These differences between 1996 and 1998 in where pupils said they drank are reflected in changes in their usual drinking companions: there was an increase in the proportion saying they were usually with their parents, and a decrease in the proportion saying they were usually with a mixed-sex group of friends.

(Tables 8.3-8.8)

8.4 **Buying alcohol**

It is against the law for anyone under 18 to buy alcohol in a pub, off-licence, shop or other outlet, but almost half of those who drink (28% of all children aged 11-15) said they did buy alcohol. Older drinkers were much more likely to buy alcohol - 78% of 11 year olds said they never did so, compared with only 34% of 15 year olds. The 1996 survey found that girls were more likely than boys to say they bought alcohol, but the opposite appeared to be the case in 1998: 49% of boys, compared with 44% of girls, said they bought alcohol.

By far the most common place of purchase was the off-licence, mentioned by 20% of drinkers. The next most frequently mentioned, by about 10% of drinkers in each case, were a shop or supermarket, a pub or bar, and a friend or relative. There were few significant differences between boys and girls in where they bought alcohol up to the age of 14. At age 15, however, gilrs were more likely to say they bought alcohol in pubs and clubs, and less likely to say they did so in off-licences or shops.

As in 1996, the 1998 data suggest that pupils are able to buy alcohol at an earlier age in shops and off-licences than in pubs and clubs. There was a marked difference between those aged 14 and those aged 15 in the proportions saying they bought drink in pubs and clubs (7% at age 14, 20% at age 15), whereas 14% of 13 year old drinkers, for example, said they bought alcohol in off-licences.

At every age, those who drank infrequently were much more likely than more frequent drinkers to say that they never bought alcohol: for example, among those aged 15, 48% of those who drank less than once a week said they never bought alcohol, compared with only 16% of those who drank at least once a week.

There was an increase in the proportion saying they never bought alcohol from 49% in 1996 to 53% in 1998, which parallels the decrease in the proportion of frequent drinkers noted earlier. Comparison of where pupils bought alcohol in

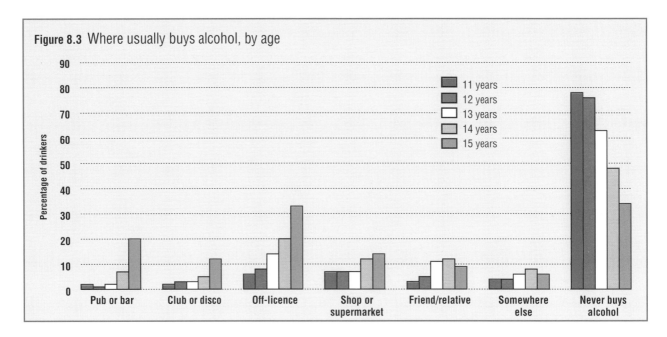

Figure 8.3 Where usually buys alcohol, by age

the two survey years is not straightforward, because an extra answer option 'friend or relative' was included in 1998. However, it appears that although there was no change in the proportions of drinkers who said they bought alcohol in pubs and clubs, there was a decrease in the proportion saying they usually bought drink in off-licences and in shops, from 27% to 20%, and from 13% to 10%, respectively.

(Tables 8.9-8.11)

Notes and references

1   The licensing laws relating to children are not straightforward. Children under 14 are not allowed in the bar of a pub unless it has a children's certificate, but they are allowed in a family room, garden, or other such area, as long as alcohol is not sold there. Those aged 14 and over (but under 18) are allowed in pubs and licensed clubs as long as they do not drink alcohol. Those aged 16 and 17 can be bought beer or cider to drink with a meal, but not in a bar.

Table 8.1 Usual drinking frequency by sex and age

All pupils   *England 1998*

Usual drinking frequency	11 years	12 years	13 years	14 years	15 years	Total
	%	%	%	%	%	%
Boys						
Almost every day	1 ⎫	2 ⎫	0 ⎫	2 ⎫	4 ⎫	2 ⎫
About twice a week	2 ⎬ 4	2 ⎬ 7	5 ⎬ 10	9 ⎬ 21	18 ⎬ 43	8 ⎬ 18
About once a week	2 ⎭	2 ⎭	5 ⎭	10 ⎭	20 ⎭	8 ⎭
About once a fortnight	2	6	8	11	11	8
About once a month	3	4	7	12	14	8
Only a few times a year	17	22	32	30	19	24
Never drinks now	6	4	6	4	4	5
Never had a drink	68	58	38	22	11	38
Base (=100%)	*287*	*335*	*294*	*601*	*741*	*2258*
	%	%	%	%	%	%
Girls						
Almost every day	0 ⎫	0 ⎫	1 ⎫	2 ⎫	1 ⎫	
About twice a week	0 ⎬ 1	1 ⎬ 5	3 ⎬ 11	10 ⎬ 21	14 ⎬ 33	6 ⎫ 14
About once a week	1 ⎭	3 ⎭	7 ⎭	10 ⎭	18 ⎭	8 ⎭
About once a fortnight	1	3	3	12	17	7
About once a month	3	4	11	12	15	9
Only a few times a year	10	25	30	28	19	23
Never drinks now	5	6	3	3	2	4
Never had a drink	80	57	42	23	14	42
Base (=100%)	*291*	*368*	*380*	*655*	*665*	*2359*
	%	%	%	%	%	%
Total						
Almost every day	0 ⎫	1 ⎫	1 ⎫	2 ⎫	3 ⎫	2 ⎫
About twice a week	1 ⎬ 3	2 ⎬ 6	4 ⎬ 11	10 ⎬ 21	16 ⎬ 38	7 ⎬ 16
About once a week	1 ⎭	3 ⎭	6 ⎭	10 ⎭	19 ⎭	8 ⎭
About once a fortnight	2	4	5	12	13	7
About once a month	3	4	10	12	14	9
Only a few times a year	13	24	31	29	19	23
Never drinks now	6	5	4	4	3	4
Never had a drink	74	57	40	22	12	40
Base (=100%)	*580*	*704*	*676*	*1254*	*1405*	*4619*

Table 8.2 Usual drinking frequency by sex: 1996 and 1998

All pupils *England*

Usual drinking frequency	1996	1998
	%	%
Boys		
Almost every day	2 ⎫	2 ⎫
About twice a week	8 ⎬ 21	8 ⎬ 18
About once a week	12 ⎭	8 ⎭
About once a fortnight	8	8
About once a month	8	8
Only a few times a year	22	24
Never drinks now	4	5
Never had a drink	37	38
Base (=100%)	*1431*	*2245*
		%
Girls		
Almost every day	2 ⎫	1 ⎫
About twice a week	7 ⎬ 18	6 ⎬ 14
About once a week	10 ⎭	8 ⎭
About once a fortnight	10	7
About once a month	9	9
Only a few times a year	21	23
Never drinks now	3	4
Never had a drink	39	42
Base (=100%)	*1387*	*2356*
		%
Total		
Almost every day	2 ⎫	2 ⎫
About twice a week	7 ⎬ 20	7 ⎬ 16
About once a week	11 ⎭	8 ⎭
About once a fortnight	9	7
About once a month	9	9
Only a few times a year	21	23
Never drinks now	4	4
Never had a drink	38	40
Base (=100%)	*2818*	*4607*

Table 8.3 Where usually drinks, by sex and age

All pupils who drink *England 1998*

Where usually drinks*	11 years	12 years	13 years	14 years	15 years	Total
	%	%	%	%	%	%
Boys						
Pub or bar	4	4	7	10	21	12
Club or disco	6	7	9	7	14	10
Parties with friends	11	18	19	25	28	23
At home, or someone else's home	76	60	61	59	55	60
Somewhere else	10	21	22	25	22	22
Base (=100%)	*93*	*146*	*183*	*475*	*668*	*1411*
	%	%	%	%	%	%
Girls						
Pub or bar	3	6	4	11	24	12
Club or disco	5	11	5	11	16	11
Parties with friends	9	11	22	27	32	24
At home, or someone else's home	84	70	56	50	47	56
Somewhere else	10	17	25	25	20	21
Base (=100%)	*66*	*164*	*227*	*519*	*578*	*1397*
	%	%	%	%	%	%
Total						
Pub or bar	4	5	6	10	22	12
Club or disco	6	9	7	9	15	10
Parties with friends	10	14	20	26	30	23
At home, or someone else's home	79	66	58	55	51	58
Somewhere else	10	19	24	25	21	21
Base (=100%)	*159*	*310*	*409*	*994*	*1245*	*2808*

*   Percentages total more than 100, because pupils could give more than one answer

Table 8.4 Who children are usually with when they drink alcohol, by sex and age

All pupils who drink   *England 1998*

Who usually drinks with*	11 years	12 years	13 years	14 years	15 years	Total
	%	%	%	%	%	%
Boys						
Girlfriend	1	5	7	6	8	6
Friends of same sex	9	12	17	19	26	19
Friends of opposite sex	3	4	3	3	6	4
Friends of both sexes	10	14	21	36	48	32
Parents	68	61	48	42	34	46
Brothers or sisters	21	14	15	16	17	16
Alone	4	5	8	3	4	5
Base (=100%)	*92*	*144*	*186*	*477*	*672*	*1415*
	%	%	%	%	%	%
Girls						
Boyfriend	2	3	4	8	14	8
Friends of same sex	8	6	21	18	16	16
Friends of opposite sex	3	2	1	6	6	4
Friends of both sexes	9	19	26	50	58	39
Parents	74	62	46	37	27	43
Brothers or sisters	23	25	14	14	14	16
Alone	4	2	1	2	2	2
Base (=100%)	*66*	*162*	*227*	*521*	*576*	*1396*
%	%	%	%	%	%	%
Total						
Boy/girlfriend	1	4	6	7	11	7
Friends of same sex	9	9	19	18	22	18
Friends of opposite sex	3	3	2	5	6	4
Friends of both sexes	10	17	24	43	53	36
Parents	70	62	47	40	31	44
Brothers or sisters	22	20	15	15	15	16
Alone	4	3	4	2	3	3
Base (=100%)	*157*	*306*	*413*	*998*	*1248*	*2811*

* Percentages total more than 100, because pupils could give more than one answer

Table 8.5 Where children usually drink, by age and usual drinking frequency

All pupils who drink   *England 1998*

Where children usually drink*	11/12 years	13 years	14 years	15 years	Total
	%	%	%	%	%
Usually drinks at least once a week					
Pub or bar	6	5	17	33	23
Club or disco	22	6	12	23	18
Parties with friends	16	20	26	27	25
At home, or someone else's home	54	58	48	52	52
Somewhere else	27	43	36	24	30
Base (=100%)	*54*	*72*	*279*	*533*	*740*
	%	%	%	%	%
Usually drinks less than once a week					
Pub or bar	5	6	8	13	8
Club or disco	6	7	8	9	8
Parties with friends	13	20	26	32	23
At home, or someone else's home	72	59	57	51	60
Somewhere else	14	19	20	18	18
Base (=100%)	403	332	698	698	2024

* Percentages total more than 100, because pupils could give more than one answer

Table 8.6 Who children usually drink with, by age and usual drinking frequency

All pupils who drink   *England 1998*

Who usually drinks with*	11/12 years	13 years	14 years	15 years	Total
	%	%	%	%	%
Usually drinks at least once a week					
Boy/girlfriend	11	14	12	16	14
Friends of same sex	18	22	19	25	22
Friends of opposite sex	3	2	10	10	8
Friends of both sexes	32	43	59	60	54
Parents	43	39	30	31	33
Brothers or sisters	16	10	13	15	14
Alone	0	2	2	4	3
Base (=100%)	*55*	*72*	*281*	*535*	*743*
	%	%	%	%	%
Usually drinks less than once a week					
Boy/girlfriend	2	4	4	6	4
Friends of same sex	8	19	18	19	16
Friends of opposite sex	3	2	3	2	3
Friends of both sexes	12	19	37	47	29
Parents	68	50	44	31	48
Brothers or sisters	21	16	16	16	17
Alone	4	4	2	2	3
Base (=100%)	*397*	*335*	*701*	*700*	*2024*

* Percentages total more than 100, because pupils could give more than one answer

Table 8.7 Where usually drinks, by sex: 1996, 1998

All pupils who drink   *England*

Where usually drinks*	1996	1998
	%	%
Boys		
Pub or bar	11	12
Club or disco	9	10
Parties with friends	23	23
At home, or someone else's home	53	60
Somewhere else	28	22
Base (=100%)	*840*	*1411*
	%	%
Girls		
Pub or bar	15	12
Club or disco	16	11
Parties with friends	24	24
At home, or someone else's home	52	56
Somewhere else	24	21
Base (=100%)	*804*	*1397*
	%	%
Total		
Pub or bar	13	12
Club or disco	13	10
Parties with friends	23	23
At home, or someone else's home	52	58
Somewhere else	26	21
Base (=100%)	*1644*	*2808*

* Percentages total more than 100, because pupils could give more than one answer

Table 8.8
Who children are usually with when they drink alcohol, by sex: 1996,1998

All pupils who drink   *England*

Who usually drinks with*	1996	1998
	%	%
Boys		
Girlfriend	5	6
Friends of same sex	18	19
Friends of opposite sex	3	4
Friends of both sexes	38	32
Parents	41	46
Brothers or sisters	15	16
Alone	4	5
Base (=100%)	*843*	*1415*
	%	%
Girls		
Boyfriend	9	8
Friends of same sex	16	16
Friends of opposite sex	4	4
Friends of both sexes	50	39
Parents	38	43
Brothers or sisters	12	16
Alone	1	2
Base (=100%)	*804*	*1396*
	%	%
Total		
Boy/girlfriend	7	7
Friends of same sex	17	18
Friends of opposite sex	4	4
Friends of both sexes	44	36
Parents	39	44
Brothers or sisters	14	16
Alone	2	3
Base (=100%)	1647	2811

* Percentages total more than 100, because pupils could give more than one answer

Table 8.9
Where children usually buy alcohol, by sex and age

All pupils who drink   *England 1998*

Where usually buys alcohol*	11 years	12 years	13 years	14 years	15 years	Total
	%	%	%	%	%	%
Boys						
Pub or bar	3	1	3	7	18	9
Club or disco	2	4	4	3	10	6
Off-licence	9	9	15	20	37	22
Shop or supermarket	8	4	6	12	16	11
Friend/relative	2	7	11	11	11	10
Somewhere else	2	7	8	10	6	7
Never buys alcohol	76	69	62	48	33	51
Base (=100%)	*97*	*148*	*188*	*474*	*670*	*1427*
	%	%	%	%	%	%
Girls						
Pub or bar	2	1	1	8	22	9
Club or disco	2	2	2	7	13	6
Off-licence	0	6	14	20	30	18
Shop or supermarket	4	9	8	12	12	10
Friend/relative	5	3	11	14	7	9
Somewhere else	7	2	5	7	7	6
Never buys alcohol	82	82	64	47	36	56
Base (=100%)	*68*	*162*	*226*	*521*	*581*	*1400*
	%	%	%	%	%	%
Total						
Pub or bar	2	1	2	7	20	9
Club or disco	2	3	3	5	12	6
Off-licence	6	8	14	20	33	20
Shop or supermarket	7	7	7	12	14	10
Friend/relative	3	5	11	12	9	9
Somewhere else	4	4	6	8	6	6
Never buys alcohol	78	76	63	48	34	53
Base (=100%)	*165*	*310*	*414*	*995*	*1251*	*2827*

*   Percentages total more than 100, because pupils could give more than one answer

Table 8.10 Where children usually buy alcohol, by age and usual drinking frequency

All pupils who drink   *England 1998*

Where usually buys alcohol*	11/12 years	13 years	14 years	15 years	Total
	%	%	%	%	%
Usually drinks at least once a week					
Pub or bar	5	3	13	31	20
Club or disco	9	3	6	18	12
Off-licence	22	29	35	49	40
Shop or supermarket	16	18	20	21	20
Friend/relative	16	20	14	10	13
Somewhere else	10	11	10	7	9
Never buys alcohol	37	34	25	16	23
Base (=100%)	*52*	*71*	*277*	*534*	*734*
	%	%	%	%	%
Usually drinks less than once a week					
Pub or bar	1	2	5	11	5
Club or disco	2	2	4	7	4
Off-licence	5	11	14	22	13
Shop or supermarket	5	5	9	9	7
Friend/relative	3	9	12	9	8
Somewhere else	3	5	7	6	5
Never buys alcohol	82	70	56	48	64
Base (=100%)	*412*	*336*	*699*	*700*	*2045*

*   Percentages total more than 100, because pupils could give more than one answer

Table 8.11
Where children usually buy alcohol, by sex: 1996,1998

All pupils who drink   *England*

Where usually buys alcohol*	1996	1998
	%	%
Boys		
Pub or bar	8	9
Club or disco	4	6
Off-licence	26	22
Shop or supermarket	12	11
Friend/relative	10	
Somewhere else	10	7
Never buys alcohol	51	51
Base (=100%)	838	1427
	%	%
Girls		
Pub or bar	12	9
Club or disco	8	6
Off-licence	28	18
Shop or supermarket	14	10
Friend/relative	9	
Somewhere else	6	6
Never buys alcohol	47	56
Base (=100%)	802	1400
	%	%
Total		
Pub or bar	10	9
Club or disco	6	6
Off-licence	27	20
Shop or supermarket	13	10
Friend/relative	9	
Somewhere else	8	6
Never buys alcohol	49	53
Base (=100%)	1640	2827

* Percentages total more than 100, because pupils could give more than one answer

9 Drug use - introduction

9.1 **Obtaining information about drug use**

In 1998 the government published a ten-year strategy to tackle drug use[1]. One of the main aims of the strategy is to help young people to resist drugs, so that they can achieve their full potential in society. It suggests that illegal drugs are becoming increasingly accessible to children and that the average age of first drug use is getting younger.

Since 1994, the British Crime Survey (BCS), a biennial survey carried out for the Home Office, has included a self-completion questionnaire on drug use for 16-59 year olds, but there has been no equivalent survey for monitoring drug use among 11-15 year olds. Thus, in 1998 the survey of smoking and drinking among secondary school children introduced questions on drug use for the first time. There were several elements to the questions:

- pupils' awareness of drugs, whether they had been offered them, and whether they had used them;
- attitudes towards the use of drugs.

The list of drugs used throughout the questions included a bogus substance called semeron. The purpose of this was to give some indication of the extent to which children were overstating their awareness of and use of drugs. To increase the accuracy of pupils' responses, the street-names of each of the drugs were included in the questions.

All pupils were asked whether they had heard of each drug on the list, and if so, whether they had ever been offered any of them. Pupils were asked whether they had ever taken any of the drugs on the list, and if they had, they were asked, for each drug, when was the last time they had done so. Finally, all pupils were asked to indicate whether they agreed or disagreed with a number of statements about drug use.

These questions were very similar to those included in the British Crime Survey, except that the 1996 BCS contained some additional questions. The list of drugs used was also very similar to the BCS list.

In some tables, data are shown for three groups of drugs, as well as for the drugs that comprise them and other drugs individually:

- stimulants: cocaine, crack, ecstasy, amphetamines, poppers;

- psychedelics: LSD, magic mushrooms (psilocybin);

- opiates: heroin, methadone.

The aim in so doing is group together drugs that, because of their similar effects, are to some extent interchangeable.

Reference

1   *Tackling drugs to build a better Britain*, Cm 3945, The Stationery Office (1998)

10 Drug use

10.1 Awareness of different drugs

Overall, pupils had a high level of awareness of drugs but 6% reported that they had never heard of any of those listed.

Awareness of the different drugs varied. Pupils were more likely to have heard of cannabis than any other drug (89%) and, despite the media attention that ecstasy attracts, they were more likely to have heard of heroin and cocaine (both 79%) than ecstasy (73%) and amphetamines, (66%). Steroids, poppers and methadone were the drugs that pupils were least aware of (38%, 37% and 33% respectively). Only 13% of children reported that they had heard of the bogus drug semeron. This is many fewer than had heard of the least known real drug, methadone, but even so, the proportion saying they had heard of it may be artificially high, since one of the street names given for semeron (bang) is, in fact, sometimes used as a name for cannabis. One quarter of all pupils said that they had heard of other drugs not included on the list. Since the list was intended to be comprehensive, it may be that they knew some drugs by other street names.

In general, girls were more likely than boys to have heard of the different types of drugs (although not all differences are statistically significant). Boys were more likely to report that they had heard of semeron, steroids, poppers and other drugs not included on the list.

Awareness of drugs increased with age. Eleven per cent of 11 year olds had heard of none of the drugs, compared with only 2% of 15 year olds, and whereas 48% of 11 year olds had heard of ecstasy, as many as 91% of 15 years olds had done so. The youngest children were more likely to have heard of drugs in the stimulants group

(76%) than of opiates (62%) and psychedelics (43%), but there was less difference in awareness of the different drug types for for older children.

(Tables 10.1-10.2)

10.2 The types of drugs pupils had been offered

About one third, 34%, of pupils had been offered at least one of the listed drugs, and the likelihood of being offered drugs increased with age (15% of 11 year olds had been offered drugs, compared with 61% of 15 year olds). Although girls were more likely than boys to have heard of drugs, they were less likely to have been offered them (32% compared with 36%). However, the difference between boys and girls was evident only among those aged 11-13: among 14 and 15 year olds, boys and girls were equally likely to have been offered drugs.

Pupils were much more likely to have been offered cannabis (26%) than any other type of drug. Even so, 14% of pupils had been offered stimulants, 8% psychedelic drugs and the same proportion, glue. Four per cent of pupils said they had been offered heroin.

Twenty-eight per cent of boys compared with 23% of girls had been offered cannabis. Except for glue, boys were also more likely than girls to have been offered each of the other drugs, but because of the comparatively small numbers, the differences were not significant.

The proportions of pupils who had been offered each individual drug increased with age: 55% of 15 year olds had been offered cannabis, for example, compared with 6% of 11 year olds.

(Figure 10.1, Tables 10.3-10.5)

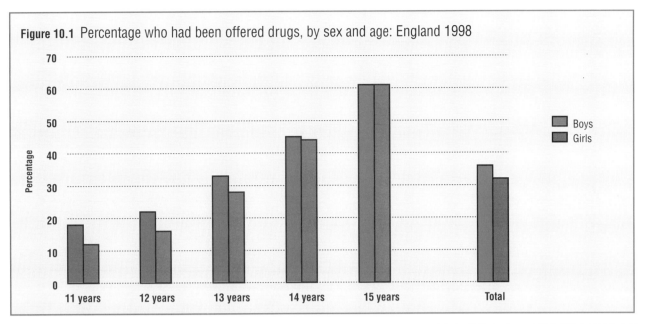

Figure 10.1 Percentage who had been offered drugs, by sex and age: England 1998

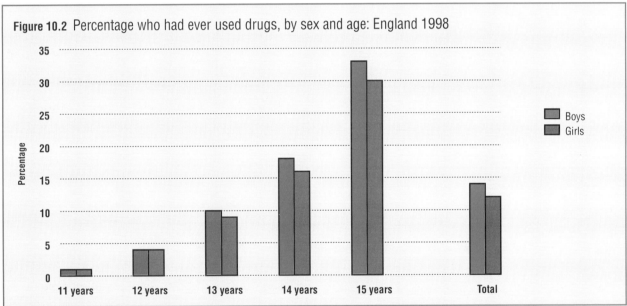

Figure 10.2 Percentage who had ever used drugs, by sex and age: England 1998

10.3 **The prevalence of drug use**

A high level of awareness and access to drugs does not necessarily imply a high level of use: only 13% of pupils had used drugs, even though 34% had been offered them. Thus the overwhelming majority of 11-15 year olds are still not taking drugs, even if given the opportunity.

The prevalence of drug use increased sharply with age: 31% of 15 year olds had used drugs compared with only 1% of 11 year olds. Boys were more likely to have used drugs than girls (14% compared with 12%) but this overall difference was contributed solely by those aged 14 and 15.

Cannabis was the individual drug that the highest proportion of pupils had used (12%), followed by amphetamines (3%). A higher proportion of pupils had used stimulants (4%) than psychedelics (2%) or opiates (1%).

Apart from cannabis, there were no significant differences between the proportions of boys and girls who had ever used individual drugs.

The proportion of pupils who had used each drug increased with age from virtually nothing at age 11. Among those aged 15, 30% of pupils had used cannabis, 12% stimulants, and 6% psychedelics, but only 1% had used opiates.

About one half of the 13% of pupils who had used drugs had only ever used one type of drug, and for many of them, drug use involved cannabis alone. Over half (52%) of those who had ever taken drugs had only used cannabis, 40% had used cannabis and other drugs, and 9% had used other drugs only (no table shown).

(Figure 10.2, Tables 10.6-10.12)

10.4 **When last used drugs**

The group of children who have ever used drugs includes those who have experimented with drugs once or twice, or use them very occasionally, as well as more regular users. This survey has no information on frequency of drug use, but pupils were asked when was the last time each drug was used.

Of the 13% of pupils who had ever used drugs, only about half - 7% of all pupils - had done so in the last month, and a further 4% of pupils had done so in the last year, though not in the last month. Two percent of pupils had last used drugs more than a year ago.

Overall, similar proportions of boys and of girls had used drugs in the last month, but among those aged 15, 19% of boys had done so, compared with 16% of girls. A total of 28% of 15 year olds had used drugs in the last year.

Half of those who had used cannabis had done so in the last month (6% of all pupils). Although not statistically significant, a higher proportion of boys than girls had used cannabis in the last month (7% compared with 5%) and the difference between the sexes was most pronounced among older pupils.

(Tables10-13-10.14)

Table 10.1 Whether had heard of individual drugs, by sex

All pupils   *England 1998*

Type of drug	Boys		Girls		Total	
Cannabis	88		89		89	
Stimulants						
Cocaine	77		80		79	
Crack	64		67		66	
Ecstasy	70	} 84	76	} 88	73	} 86
Amphetamines	66		66		66	
Poppers	38		36		37	
Psychedelics						
LSD	64	} 71	64	} 73	64	} 72
Magic mushrooms	61		63		62	
Opiates						
Heroin	76	} 76	82	} 83	79	} 80
Methadone	31		36		33	
Tranquilisers	47		50		48	
Steroids	42		34		38	
Semeron	15		12		13	
Other drugs	28		23		25	
Never heard of any of the drugs	6		5		6	
Base (=100%)	2335		2416		4751	

Table 10.2 Whether had heard of individual drugs, by age

All pupils   *England 1998*

Type of drug	11 years	12 years	13 years	14 years	15 years	Total
Cannabis	72	88	90	94	97	89
Stimulants						
Cocaine	63	71	80	86	92	79
Crack	37	56	67	79	86	66
Ecstasy	48 } 76	63 } 81	75 } 87	83 } 91	91 } 95	73 } 86
Amphetamines	38	51	69	80	88	66
Poppers	11	20	32	52	66	37
Psychedelics						
LSD	31 } 43	49 } 61	66 } 75	80 } 85	89 } 92	64 } 72
Magic mushrooms	30	47	62	77	88	62
Opiates						
Heroin	61 } 62	73 } 74	81 } 82	86 } 86	91 } 92	79 } 80
Methadone	15	24	32	41	52	33
Tranquilisers	25	35	47	60	71	48
Steroids	18	27	36	47	60	38
Semeron	8	9	12	16	21	13
Other drugs	19	22	22	30	32	25
Never heard of any of the drugs	11	7	6	3	2	6
Base (=100%)	*612*	*728*	*696*	*1284*	*1430*	*4751*

Table 10.3 Whether had been offered drugs by sex and age

All pupils   *England 1998*

	11 years	12 years	13 years	14 years	15 years	Total
	Percentage who had been offered drugs					
Boys	18	22	33	45	61	36
Girls	12	16	28	44	61	32
Total	15	19	30	44	61	34
Bases (=100%)						
Boys	*306*	*353*	*306*	*612*	*757*	*2334*
Girls	*305*	*374*	*390*	*672*	*674*	*2415*
Total	*612*	*728*	*696*	*1284*	*1430*	*4750*

Table 10.4 Whether had been offered individual drugs, by sex

All pupils   *England 1998*

Type of drug	Boys	Girls	Total
Cannabis	28	23	26
Stimulants			
Cocaine	6	5	6
Crack	4	2	3
Ecstasy	7 } 15	5 } 13	6 } 14
Amphetamines	8	7	7
Poppers	6	5	6
Psychedelics			
LSD	7 } 9	5 } 7	6 } 8
Magic Mushrooms	6	5	6
Opiates			
Heroin	4 } 5	3 } 3	4 } 4
Methadone	2	1	1
Glue	8	9	8
Tranquilisers	3	2	2
Steroids	2	1	2
Semeron	2	0	1
Other drugs	6	5	6
Total offered any drug	36	32	34
Base (=100%)	*2335*	*2416*	*4751*

Table 10.5 Whether had been offered individual drugs, by age

All pupils   *England 1998*

Type of drug	11 years	12 years	13 years	14 years	15 years	Total
Cannabis	6	10	19	36	55	26
Stimulants						
Cocaine	4	3	4	6	10	6
Crack	2	2	3	4	6	3
Ecstasy	2	3	4	7	13	6
Amphetamines	2	2	5	9	18	7
Poppers	1	1	4	7	14	6
(grouped)	7	6	10	17	30	14
Psychedelics						
LSD	2	2	3	8	13	6
Magic Mushrooms	2	2	4	7	13	6
(grouped)	3	3	5	11	18	8
Opiates						
Heroin	3	2	4	4	6	4
Methadone	0	1	1	1	2	1
(grouped)	3	2	4	4	6	4
Glue	4	6	9	10	13	8
Tranquilisers	1	2	2	2	4	2
Steroids	1	1	2	2	3	2
Semeron	1	1	1	1	2	1
Other drugs	3	4	6	7	8	6
Total offered any drug	15	19	30	44	61	34
Base (=100%)	*612*	*727*	*696*	*1284*	*1430*	*4749*

Table 10.6 Percentage who had ever used drugs by sex and age

All pupils   *England 1998*

	11 years	12 years	13 years	14 years	15 years	Total
	Percentage who had ever used drugs					
Boys	1	4	10	18	33	14
Girls	1	4	9	16	30	12
Total	1	5	9	18	31	13
Bases (=100%)						
Boys	*305*	*353*	*303*	*610*	*756*	*2327*
Girls	*305*	*373*	*388*	*671*	*674*	*2411*
Total	*610*	*727*	*692*	*1282*	*1430*	*4741*

Table 10.7 Percentage who had ever used individual drugs, by sex

All pupils

Type of drug	Boys	Girls	Total
	Percentage who had ever used the drug		
Cannabis	13	11	12
Stimulants			
Cocaine	1	1	1
Crack	0	0	0
Ecstasy	1	0	1
Amphetamines	2	3	3
Poppers	2	2	2
(grouped)	4	4	4
Psychedelics			
LSD	1	1	1
Magic mushrooms	2	2	2
(grouped)	2	2	2
Opiates			
Heroin	0	0	0
Methadone	0	0	0
(grouped)	1	1	1
Glue	2	2	2
Tranquilisers	1	0	0
Steroids	0	0	0
Semeron	0	0	0
Other drugs	1	2	1
Total who had ever used any of the above	14	12	13
Base (=100%)	*2289*	*2360*	*4649*

Table 10.8 Percentage who had ever used individual drugs, by age

All pupils   *England 1998*

Type of drug	11 years		12 years		13 years		14 years		15 years		Total (all ages)	
Cannabis	1		2		8		16		30		12	
Stimulants												
Cocaine	0		0		0		1		2		1	
Crack	0		0		0		0		1		0	
Ecstasy	0	} 0	0	} 1	0	} 2	1	} 6	2	} 12	1	} 4
Amphetamines	0		0		2		3		8		3	
Poppers	0		0		0		3		6		2	
Psychedelics												
LSD	0	} 0	0	} 0	0	} 1	2	} 3	3	} 6	1	} 2
Magic mushrooms	0		0		1		3		5		2	
Opiates												
Heroin	0	} 0	0	} 0	0	} 1	1	} 1	0	} 1	0	} 1
Methadone	0		0		0		0		1		0	
Glue	0		1		1		3		6		2	
Tranquilisers	0		0		0		1		2		1	
Steroids	0		0		0		1		1		0	
Semeron	0		0		0		0		0		0	
Others	0		0		1		2		4		1	
Total who had ever used any drug	1		5		11		19		33		13	
Base (=100%)	*610*		*727*		*690*		*1282*		*1429*		*4648*	

Table 10.9 Percentage who had ever used cannabis by sex and age

All pupils   *England 1998*

	11 years	12 years	13 years	14 years	15 years	Total
	Percentage who had ever used cannabis					
Boys	1	3	8	17	31	13
Girls	1	2	8	16	30	11
Total	1	2	8	17	30	12
Bases (=100%)						
Boys	*305*	*353*	*303*	*611*	*755*	*2327*
Girls	*305*	*373*	*387*	*670*	*674*	*2409*
Total	*610*	*727*	*690*	*1282*	*1429*	*4738*

Table 10.10 Percentage who had ever used stimulants by sex and age

All pupils   *England 1998*

	11 years	12 years	13 years	14 years	15 years	Total
	Percentage who had ever used stimulants					
Boys	0	1	1	6	12	4
Girls	0	1	3	6	12	4
Total	0	1	2	6	12	4
Bases (=100%)						
Boys	*370*	*353*	*305*	*613*	*756*	*2334*
Girls	*305*	*374*	*390*	*671*	*674*	*2414*
Total	*612*	*728*	*696*	*1284*	*1430*	*4750*

Table 10.11 Percentage who had ever used psychedelics by sex and age

All pupils   *England 1998*

	11 years	12 years	13 years	14 years	15 years	Total
	Percentage who had ever used psychedelics					
Boys	0	0	0	3	7	2
Girls	0	1	1	3	5	2
Total	0	0	1	3	6	2
Bases (=100%)						
Boys	*306*	*353*	*306*	*613*	*756*	*2334*
Girls	*305*	*374*	*390*	*671*	*674*	*2414*
Total	*612*	*728*	*696*	*1284*	*1430*	*4750*

Table 10.12 Percentage who had ever used opiates by sex and age

All pupils   *England 1998*

	11 years	12 years	13 years	14 years	15 years	Total
	Percentage who had ever used opiates					
Boys	0	0	1	1	1	1
Girls	0	0	1	1	2	1
Total	0	0	1	1	1	1
Bases (=100%)						
Boys	*307*	*353*	*306*	*613*	*757*	*2336*
Girls	*305*	*375*	*390*	*671*	*674*	*2415*
Total	*612*	*728*	*695*	*1284*	*1430*	*4749*

Table 10.13 When last used drugs, by sex and age

All pupils   *England 1998*

	11 years	12 years	13 years	14 years	15 years	Total
	%	%	%	%	%	%
Boys						
In the last month	0	2	4	10	19	7
In the last year	1	2	3	6	10	5
More than a year ago	0	1	3	2	4	2
Never used drugs	99	96	90	81	67	86
Base (=100%)	*305*	*352*	*304*	*610*	*757*	*2328*
	%	%	%	%	%	%
Girls						
In the last month	0	2	3	9	16	6
In the last year	1	1	3	5	10	4
More than a year ago	0	1	2	2	4	2
Never used drugs	99	96	91	84	70	88
Base (=100%)	*305*	*373*	*388*	*671*	*674*	*2411*
	%	%	%	%	%	%
Total						
In the last month	0	2	4	10	18	7
In the last year	1	2	3	6	10	4
More than a year ago	0	1	2	2	4	2
Never used drugs	99	96	91	82	69	87
Base (=100%)	*610*	*727*	*692*	*1281*	*1431*	*4741*

Table 10.14 When last used cannabis, by sex and age

All pupils   *England 1998*

	11 years		12 years		13 years		14 years		15 years		Total	
	%		%		%		%		%		%	
Boys												
In the last month	0		1		2		10		18		7	
In the last year	0	}1	1	}3	3	}8	5	}17	10	}31	4	}13
More than a year ago	0		1		3		2		4		2	
Never used cannabis	99		97		92		83		69		87	
Base (=100%)	*305*		*353*		*304*		*612*		*755*		*2329*	
	%		%		%		%		%		%	
Girls												
In the last month	0		0		3		8		13		5	
In the last year	1	}1	1	}2	3	}8	5	}16	11	}28	4	}11
More than a year ago	0		1		2		3		4		2	
Never used cannabis	99		98		92		84		72		89	
Base (=100%)	*305*		*373*		*386*		*670*		*674*		*2408*	
	%		%		%		%		%		%	
Total												
In the last month	0		1		3		9		16		6	
In the last year	1	}1	1	}3	3	}8	5	}16	10	}30	4	}12
More than a year ago	0		1		2		2		4		2	
Never used cannabis	99		98		92		84		70		88	
Base (=100%)	*610*		*727*		*690*		*1281*		*1428*		*4736*	

11 Attitudes to drug use

11.1 Attitudes to drug use

Pupils were asked to indicate whether or not they agreed with each of ten attitude statements. The statement that was agreed with by the highest proportion of pupils was 'taking drugs harms your health' (91%) followed by 'people who take drugs are stupid' (71%). The statement that the smallest proportion of pupils agreed with was 'drugs are not as harmful as people say' (8%). One of the key objectives of the government's drugs strategy is to increase childrens' levels of knowledge about the risks of taking drugs. Only 27% of pupils agreed with the statement 'I don't know enough about the danger of drugs' but this does not necessarily imply that children are well-informed - they may just be ignorant.

Overall, boys were more likely than girls to have a positive attitude towards drug use. A higher proportion of boys than girls agreed with the statements 'taking drugs is exciting' (13% compared with 7%) and 'people take drugs to relax' (44% compared with 37%). On the whole,

however, boys as well as girls expressed negative attitudes towards drug use.

Younger children were more likely than older children to express negative attitudes towards drug use: for example, 82% of 11 year olds agreed with the statement 'people who take drugs are stupid' compared with only 53% of 15 year olds. It is interesting that at each age, the overwhelming majority of pupils agreed with the statement 'taking drugs harms your health'.

As might be expected, those pupils who had used drugs were more likely to have positive attitudes towards drug use than those who had never done so. For example, 43% of pupils who had used drugs agreed with the statement 'taking drugs is exciting' compared with only 5% of pupils who had never tried drugs. Also, a much higher proportion of pupils who had taken drugs agreed with the statements 'most young people will try out drugs at some time (88% compared with 52%) and 'I know people my age who take drugs' (88% compared with 38%).

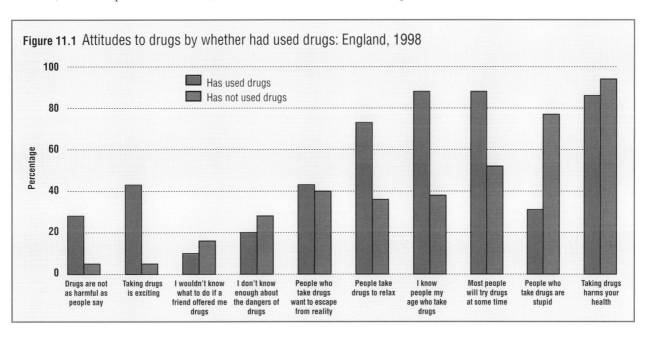

Figure 11.1 Attitudes to drugs by whether had used drugs: England, 1998

Despite the differences between those who had taken drugs and those who had not, the majority of pupils who had used drugs nonetheless agreed with the statement 'taking drugs harms your health' (86%). This suggests that awareness of the risks of drugs does not necessarily stop people from using them.

Among those who had taken drugs, boys were more likely to have positive attitudes towards drug use than girls. Forty-nine per cent of boys who had taken drugs agreed with the statement 'taking drugs is exciting' compared with 36% of girls, and only 20% of girls who had used drugs agreed with the statement 'drugs are not as harmful as people say they are' compared with 36% of boys.

(Tables 11.1- 11.3)

Table 11.1 Attitudes to drugs, by sex

All pupils			England 1998
Proportion of pupils who agreed with each statement	Boys	Girls	Total
	Percentage who agreed		
Drugs are not as harmful as people say they are	11	5	8
Taking drugs is exciting	13	7	10
I wouldn't know what to do if a friend offered me drugs	15	16	16
I don't know enough about the danger of drugs	26	29	27
People who take drugs want to escape from reality	38	41	40
People take drugs to relax	44	37	41
I know people my age who take drugs	43	45	44
Most people will try out drugs at some time	58	55	57
People who take drugs are stupid	70	72	71
Taking drugs harms your health	90	93	91
Base (=100%)	2188	2296	4484

Table 11.2 Attitudes to drugs, by age

All pupils						England 1998
Proportion of pupils who agreed with each statement	11 years	12 years	13 years	14 years	15 years	Total
	Percentage who agreed					
Drugs are not as harmful as people say they are	3	5	7	11	13	8
Taking drugs is exciting	1	4	8	16	20	10
I wouldn't know what to do if a friend offered me drugs	18	19	16	14	10	16
I don't know enough about the danger of drugs	33	29	29	24	22	27
People who take drugs want to escape from reality	37	36	44	42	38	40
People take drugs to relax	30	34	39	48	50	41
I know people my age who take drugs	12	20	39	63	79	44
Most people will try out drugs at some time	42	45	57	65	71	57
People who take drugs are stupid	82	83	74	64	53	71
Taking drugs harms your health	91	94	92	92	90	92
Base (=100%)	555	670	668	1230	1387	4510

Table 11.3 Attitudes to drugs by whether had ever used them, by sex

All pupils   *England 1998*

	Used drugs	Never used drugs	Total
	% who agreed with each statement		
Boys			
Drugs are not as harmful as people say they are	36	7	11
Taking drugs is exciting	49	7	14
I wouldn't know what to do if a friend offered me drugs	11	16	15
I don't know enough about the danger of drugs	19	27	26
People who take drugs want to escape from reality	40	38	38
People take drugs to relax	76	39	45
I know people my age who take drugs	85	36	44
Most people will try out drugs at some time	90	53	59
People who take drugs are stupid	32	76	69
Taking drugs harms your health	83	93	91
Base (=100%)	*315*	*1693*	*2008*
Girls			
Drugs are not as harmful as people say they are	20	3	5
Taking drugs is exciting	36	4	8
I wouldn't know what to do if a friend offered me drugs	8	17	16
I don't know enough about the danger of drugs	21	30	29
People who take drugs want to escape from reality	45	42	42
People take drugs to relax	70	34	38
I know people my age who take drugs	92	40	46
Most people will try out drugs at some time	87	52	56
People who take drugs are stupid	29	77	71
Taking drugs harms your health	88	95	94
Base (=100%)	*283*	*1852*	*2135*
Total			
Drugs are not as harmful as people say they are	28	5	8
Taking drugs is exciting	43	5	11
I wouldn't know what to do if a friend offered me drugs	10	16	15
I don't know enough about the danger of drugs	20	28	27
People who take drugs want to escape from reality	43	40	40
People take drugs to relax	73	36	42
I know people my age who take drugs	88	38	45
Most people will try out drugs at some time	88	52	58
People who take drugs are stupid	31	77	70
Taking drugs harms your health	86	94	93
Base (=100%)	*603*	*3538*	*4141*

12 Smoking, drinking and drug use

12.1 Introduction

Previous chapters in this report have considered smoking, drinking and drug use each in isolation. To summarise very briefly the information presented, the prevalence of all three behaviours increases steeply with age. Girls are more likely than boys to be smokers, but boys are more likely to drink, they have higher alcohol consumption, and they are more likely than girls to have taken drugs.

There is considerable interest in the extent to which children who smoke or drink are more likely than other children to experiment with drugs or become regular drug users. It is not possible with the data obtained from this survey to look at the order in which children take up these behaviours - a longitudinal survey would be needed, in which the same group of children were interviewed several times over a period of years. However, we do know from the survey that at age 15, about three fifths of all pupils have had an alcoholic drink, two fifths have tried smoking, and just over one in ten have used drugs. Consideration of the association between three variables is complex, so the relationship between smoking and drinking is considered first.

12.2 Smoking and drinking

Surveys such as the General Household Survey (GHS) have shown that there is a clear association between smoking and drinking among adult men and women. Data from the 1996 GHS show, for example, that 11% of men who were current smokers drank on average more than 50 units a week, compared with only 3% of men who had never smoked, and that men

in the highest alcohol consumption category were twice as likely as non-drinkers to be current smokers[1].

A similar association for 11-15 year old children is shown in Tables 12.1 and 12.2. The association between smoking and drinking can be analysed in two ways: either smoking or drinking may be treated as the 'independent' variable across which differences in the other 'dependent' variable may be compared. Table 12.1 shows how smoking behaviour varies according to frequency of drinking. Overall, 11% of pupils were regular smokers, but the proportion ranged from 1% of those who had never had a drink, to as many as 36% of those who usually drank every week. Variation in smoking prevalence according to usual drinking frequency appeared to be greater for girls than for boys, probably because the prevalence of smoking is higher among girls. More than three quarters of those who had never had an alcoholic drink had never smoked.

This variation in smoking according to drinking does not necessarily imply that the reverse is also true, but Table 12.2 indeed shows that there was also considerable variation in usual drinking frequency according to smoking behaviour: 55% of regular smokers, but only 5% of those who had never smoked, said they usually drank at least once a week. Only 5% of regular smokers had never had an alcoholic drink.

This association between smoking and drinking is not simply due to the fact that the prevalence of both behaviours increases with age. Among 15 year olds, for example, 60% of regular smokers, but only 18% of those who had never smoked, said they usually drank at least once a week. Similarly, the proportion of pupils aged 15 who were regular smokers ranged from 7% of those who did not drink, to 38% of those who usually drank every week. Table 12.4 condenses the combinations of smoking behaviour and drinking frequency shown in Table 12.3 so that differences between boys and girls and between pupils of different ages can be shown. The proportion of pupils who are regular smokers who usually drink every week rises from fewer than 0.5% at age 11 to 14% at age 15. Conversely, the proportion who have never tried smoking and do not drink at all falls from 68% of 11 year olds to just 9% of 15 year olds.

(Tables 12.1-12.4)

12.3 Drug use in relation to smoking and drinking

The likelihood of having ever used drugs is very strongly related to smoking experience: 63% of regular smokers had used drugs, compared with only 1% of those who had never smoked. In each category of smoking behaviour, boys were more likely than girls to have used drugs, and older pupils were more likely than younger ones to have done so. The difference in relation to age was least marked for regular smokers. There were few pupils aged 11/12 who were regular smokers, but among those aged 13 and over, the proportion of regular smokers who had used drugs rose only from 61% at age 13 to 69% at age 15, compared with an increase among all pupils from 9% at age 13 to 31% at age 15.

Drug use was also related to usual drinking frequency, but a little less strongly than in relation to smoking - 44% of those who drank at least once a week had used drugs, compared with only 1% of those who had never had a drink. Within each category of drinking behaviour, there were no significant differences between boys and girls in the prevalence of drug use. As with smoking, in each drinking category, the older pupils were, the more likely they were to have used drugs.

Table 12.9 shows drug use in relation to the different combinations of smoking and drinking behaviour. Virtually no children who had never smoked or drunk alcohol had ever used drugs, but as many as three quarters of regular smokers who drank at least once a week had done so. This table also confirms the suggestion made above

that drug use is more closely associated with smoking than with drinking. The data from this survey can throw no light directly on why this is so, but one possible explanation is the finding discussed in Chapter 10 that about 90% of drug users aged 11-15 had used cannabis, which is usually smoked.

(Tables 12.5-12.9)

12.4 Assessing the relative importance of different factors in determining whether children are likely to have used drugs

This chapter has shown that smoking, drinking and drug use are closely associated. All three behaviours also vary according to sex, though not always in the same way (for example, girls are more likely to smoke, but boys are more likely to have used drugs) and age (the likelihood of all three behaviours increases with age).

To examine the interactions between these factors, loglinear modelling[2] has been used to examine the relative importance of sex, age, smoking behaviour and usual drinking frequency in predicting whether or not a child had ever used drugs. It should be noted that although the survey has shown that all these characteristics are associated with drug use, there are likely to be many other factors involved which have not been covered by the survey.

Each of the four variables made a significant contribution to the variation in the outcome variable (whether or not the child had ever used drugs) after all the other characteristics had been controlled for. Thus, for example, the association between drug use and age is not solely due to the fact that drug use is associated with smoking and drinking, both of which characteristics are associated with age. However, as suggested by the crosstabulations discussed earlier, smoking behaviour was clearly the most important factor in predicting whether or not a pupil had used drugs.

(Table 12.10)

Notes and references

1   See Tables 10.34-10.37 in *Living in Britain: Results from the 1996 General Household Survey* The Stationery Office (1998)

2   See technical annex below

Technical annex

Odds ratios and logistic regression

The odds of an event happening are related to its probability (p) in the following way:

$$odds = p/(1-p).$$

To take an example, 63% of regular smokers and 24% of occasional smokers had used drugs. The odds of doing so are thus 63/37 for regular smokers and 24/76 for occasional smokers, and the relative odds (sometimes referred to as the odds ratio) of a regular smoker having taken drugs, compared with an occasional smoker, are (63/37)/(24/76), or about 5.4 to 1. The ratio of percentages is smaller, 2.6, and the odds ratio is different because it depends on the absolute, as well as the relative size of the percentages (or probabilities).

Although odds ratios are difficult to interpret, the technique of logistic regression is valuable because it indicates whether each variable makes a significant contribution to explaining variation in the outcome variables, having held all other variables under consideration constant. Table 12.10 shows, for each characteristic, the odds of having used drugs relative to a reference category (for example, pupils aged 11 for the age variable), and the 95% confidence interval. All the odds ratios shown are significantly different from 1, the value for the reference category. (If the confidence interval contained the value 1.00, the difference from the reference category would not be statistically significant.)

Table 12.1 Smoking behaviour, by sex and usual drinking frequency

All pupils   *England 1998*

Smoking behaviour	Usual drinking frequency						
	Every week	Once a fortnight	Once a month	A few times a year	Don't drink now	Never had a drink	Total
Boys	%	%	%	%	%	%	%
Regular smoker	29	14	10	4	5	2	9
Occasional smoker	15	14	9	6	8	4	8
Used to smoke	16	16	12	12	7	3	9
Tried smoking	21	26	27	22	32	14	20
Never smoked	19	31	42	55	48	78	54
Base(=100%)	*408*	*171*	*186*	*532*	*101*	*832*	*2230*
Girls							
Regular smoker	46	30	18	6	8	1	12
Occasional smoker	14	16	18	10	3	3	9
Used to smoke	17	18	19	14	6	4	10
Tried smoking	10	16	22	25	20	15	18
Never smoked	14	19	23	46	62	77	51
Base(=100%)	*334*	*170*	*220*	*545*	*93*	*992*	*2354*
Total							
Regular smoker	36	21	14	5	6	1	11
Occasional smoker	15	15	14	8	5	3	8
Used to smoke	16	17	16	13	7	3	10
Tried smoking	16	22	24	24	26	14	19
Never smoked	16	25	32	50	55	77	52
Base(=100%)	*742*	*341*	*404*	*1077*	*194*	*1823*	*4581*

Table 12.2 Usual drinking frequency, by sex and smoking behaviour

All pupils   *England 1998*

Smoking behaviour		Usual drinking frequency						
		Every week	Once a fortnight	Once a month	A few times a year	Don't drink now	Never had a drink	*Base=100%*
Boys								
Regular smoker	%	59	11	9	11	2	7	*202*
Occasional smoker	%	35	13	9	19	5	18	*173*
Used to smoke	%	31	13	11	30	3	12	*209*
Tried smoking	%	19	10	11	27	7	25	*448*
Never smoked	%	6	4	7	24	4	54	*1198*
Total	%	18	8	8	24	4	37	*2230*
Girls								
Regular smoker	%	52	18	13	11	2	4	*292*
Occasional smoker	%	24	13	20	26	2	15	*202*
Used to smoke	%	23	13	17	31	2	14	*246*
Tried smoking	%	8	7	12	32	5	36	*414*
Never smoked	%	4	3	4	21	5	64	*1200*
Total	%	14	7	9	23	4	42	*2354*
Total								
Regular smoker	%	55	15	11	11	2	5	*492*
Occasional smoker	%	30	13	15	23	3	17	*373*
Used to smoke	%	26	13	14	30	3	14	*457*
Tried smoking	%	14	9	12	30	6	31	*862*
Never smoked	%	5	4	5	23	4	59	*2397*
Total	%	16	7	9	24	4	40	*4581*

Table 12.3 Smoking behaviour and usual drinking frequency

Pupils aged 15   *England 1998*

Smoking behaviour	Usual drinking frequency					
	Every week	Once a fortnight	Once a month	A few times a year	Doesn't drink	Total
(a) smoking behaviour by usual drinking frequency						
	%	%	%	%	%	%
Regular smoker	38	30	20	8	7	24
Occasional smoker	13	15	12	7	2	10
Used to smoke	20	14	16	14	6	15
Tried smoking	14	22	21	25	22	20
Never smoked	14	19	31	46	63	31
Base (=100%)	*592*	*210*	*224*	*302*	*245*	*1573*
(b) usual drinking frequency by smoking behaviour						*Base (=100%)*
	%	%	%	%	%	%
Regular smoker	60	17	12	7	4	375
Occasional smoker	49	19	16	13	2	161
Used to smoke	48	12	15	18	7	243
Tried smoking	28	15	15	24	18	307
Never smoked	18	8	14	28	32	487
Total	38	13	14	19	16	1573

Table 12.4 Smoking behaviour and usual drinking frequency, by sex and age

All pupils   *England 1998*

Smoking behaviour	Age 11 years	12 years	13 years	14 years	15 years	Total
Boys	%	%	%	%	%	%
Regular smoker:						
drinks every week	0	1	2	8	13	5
drinks less than weekly	1	2	0	6	5	3
does not drink at all	0	0	2	1	1	1
Ex-smokers, occasional smokers:						
drinks every week	3	4	5	10	22	10
drinks less than weekly	6	14	22	24	21	18
does not drink at all	12	12	15	8	4	10
Has never smoked:						
drinks every week	1	2	3	3	7	3
drinks less than weekly	15	16	25	22	18	19
does not drink at all	62	49	26	17	9	31
Base(=100%)	*280*	*332*	*292*	*598*	*737*	*2239*
Girls	%	%	%	%	%	%
Regular smoker:						
drinks every week	0	1	5	10	16	6
drinks less than weekly	1	1	4	8	12	5
does not drink at all	0	1	1	1	1	1
Ex-smokers, occasional smokers:						
drinks every week	0	3	4	8	14	6
drinks less than weekly	5	15	25	28	26	20
does not drink at all	11	14	14	8	5	10
Has never smoked:						
drinks every week	0	1	2	3	4	2
drinks less than weekly	8	16	15	17	13	14
does not drink at all	74	49	30	18	10	35
Base(=100%)	*289*	*368*	*381*	*655*	*665*	*2358*
Total	%	%	%	%	%	%
Regular smoker:						
drinks every week	0	1	4	9	14	6
drinks less than weekly	1	1	2	7	8	4
does not drink at all	0	1	1	1	1	1
Ex-smokers, occasional smokers:						
drinks every week	2	3	5	9	18	8
drinks less than weekly	6	15	24	26	23	19
does not drink at all	11	13	14	8	4	10
Has never smoked:						
drinks every week	1	2	2	3	6	3
drinks less than weekly	12	16	19	20	16	17
does not drink at all	68	49	28	17	9	33
Base(=100%)	*571*	*698*	*675*	*1253*	*1401*	*4598*

Table 12.5 Drug use by smoking behaviour by sex

All pupils   *England 1998*

Smoking behaviour	Boys	Girls	Total
	percentage who had used drugs		
Regular smoker	66	60	63
Occasional smoker	29	20	24
Used to smoke	32	18	24
Tried smoking	10	4	7
Never smoked	2	1	1
Total	14	12	13
Bases=100%)			
Regular smoker	*209*	*295*	*505*
Occasional smoker	*175*	*203*	*378*
Used to smoke	*212*	*250*	*460*
Tried smoking	*460*	*423*	*882*
Never smoked	*1250*	*1238*	*2488*
Total	*2306*	*2409*	*4713*

Table 12.6 Drug use by age and smoking behaviour

All pupils   *England 1998*

Smoking behaviour	Age 11/12 years	13 years	14 years	15 years	Total
	percentage who had used drugs				
Regular smoker	[30]	61	62	69	63
Occasional smoker	9	19	20	43	24
Used to smoke	18	17	17	38	24
Tried smoking	3	3	8	16	7
Never smoked	0	0	3	4	1
Total	3	9	18	31	13
Bases=100%)					
Regular smoker	*27*	*50*	*229*	*342*	*505*
Occasional smoker	*61*	*61*	*141*	*154*	*378*
Used to smoke	*55*	*87*	*157*	*217*	*460*
Tried smoking	*216*	*143*	*256*	*277*	*882*
Never smoked	*965*	*347*	*496*	*437*	*2488*
Total	*1324*	*688*	*1279*	*1427*	*4713*

Table 12.7 Drug use by usual drinking frequency by sex

All pupils   *England 1998*

Usual drinking frequency	Boys	Girls	Total
	percentage who had used drugs		
At least once a week	42	46	44
About once a fortnight	25	28	27
About once a month	18	15	16
Only a few times a year	9	6	8
Never drinks now	9	4	7
Never had a drink	2	1	1
Total	14	12	13
Bases=100%)			
At least once a week	*409*	*335*	*744*
About once a fortnight	*172*	*170*	*342*
About once a month	*185*	*221*	*406*
Only a few times a year	*530*	*546*	*1076*
Never drinks now	*103*	*91*	*194*
Never had a drink	*844*	*991*	*1836*
Total	*2243*	*2354*	*4598*

Table 12.8 Drug use by age and usual drinking frequency

All pupils   *England 1998*

Usual drinking frequency	Age 11/12 years	13 years	14 years	15 years	Total
	percentage who had used drugs				
At least once a week	16	35	46	51	44
About once a fortnight	[16]	[20]	23	37	27
About once a month	[0]	12	19	26	16
Only a few times a year	4	7	8	14	8
Never drinks now	3	[5]	[12]	[14]	7
Never had a drink	1	2	2	3	1
Total	3	9	18	32	13
Bases=100%)					
At least once a week	*55*	*72*	*280*	*536*	*744*
About once a fortnight	*37*	*36*	*149*	*189*	*342*
About once a month	*48*	*63*	*150*	*202*	*406*
Only a few times a year	*243*	*206*	*356*	*268*	*1076*
Never drinks now	*68*	*28*	*45*	*42*	*194*
Never had a drink	*830*	*266*	*273*	*169*	*1836*
Total	*1281*	*671*	*1253*	*1406*	*4598*

Table 12.9 Drug use by smoking behaviour and usual drinking frequency

All pupils   *England 1998*

Smoking behaviour	Usual drinking frequency					
	Every week	Once a fortnight	Once a month	A few times a year*	Never had a drink	Total
	percentage who had ever used drugs					
Regular smoker	75	60	57	39	[20]	63
Occasional smoker	42	28	24	13	8	24
Used to smoke	38	34	19	18	8	24
Tried smoking	20	9	7	6	2	7
Never smoked	6	6	2	2	0	1
Total	44	26	17	7	1	13
Base=100%						
Regular smoker	*271*	*73*	*56*	*67*	*25*	*492*
Occasional smoker	*110*	*50*	*55*	*96*	*62*	*373*
Used to smoke	*120*	*58*	*64*	*153*	*62*	*457*
Tried smoking	*120*	*74*	*99*	*305*	*264*	*862*
Never smoked	*121*	*86*	*130*	*650*	*1410*	*2397*
Total	*742*	*341*	*404*	*1271*	*1823*	*4581*

* includes those who said they used to drink but did not do so now

Table 12.10 Results of fitted logit model

All pupils

	Number in sample	Relative odds	95% confidence interval
General effect		0.12	0.09 - 0.14
Sex			
Boy	*2335*	1.69	1.35 - 2.12
Girl	*2417*	1.00	
Age			
11	*611*	1.00	
12	*728*	2.79	1.18 - 6.60
13	*696*	3.62	1.58 - 8.31
14	*1283*	3.94	1.73 - 8.95
15	*1431*	6.58	2.92 - 14.85
Smoking behaviour			
Regular smoker	*505*	46.70	30.46 - 71.47
Occasional smoker	*379*	11.35	7.24 - 17.79
Used to smoke	*464*	11.19	7.24 - 17.28
Tried smoking	*887*	3.49	2.22 - 5.49
Never smoked	*2490*	1.00	
Usual drinking frequency			
At least once a week	*744*	7.20	4.51 - 11.47
About once a fortnight	*341*	4.79	2.87 - 8.01
About once a month	*407*	3.23	1.92 - 5.45
Only a few times a year	*1078*	2.47	1.52 - 4.01
Never drinks now	*196*	2.56	1.21 - 5.45
Never had a drink	*1840*	1.00	

13 Health education in school

13.1 Introduction

Since 1986, pupils have been asked if they could remember having had classes in the previous year covering health education issues. In 1986, they were asked only about lessons on smoking, dental health, healthy eating, and drugs. Additional topics were added in subsequent surveys, and in 1998, they were given a list of thirteen topics on which health education might have been given, and asked to say if they remembered having any lessons on each of these in the last year. The topics asked about in 1998 were as follows:

- smoking;
- dental health;
- healthy eating;
- drugs;
- alcohol;
- AIDS;
- solvents;
- exercise/sports;
- sunbathing/sunburn risks;
- sex education/safe sex;
- heroin;
- crack;
- ecstasy.

It should be noted that pupils completed the questionnaires in the autumn of 1998. Thus, for most of the period referred to in the question (the last year), pupils were one school year lower than at the time of fieldwork - and most year 7 pupils would have been at primary school.

13.2 Health education lessons in the last year

In 1998, a higher percentage of pupils remembered receiving lessons on smoking and on healthy eating than on any other topics. The proportion of pupils who remembered receiving health education on smoking has almost doubled since 1986, having risen from 42% then to 78% in 1998. In previous years, a higher percentage of pupils had recalled lessons on healthy eating than on smoking but in 1998, equal proportions of pupils remembered having lessons on each. Although fewer pupils remembered health education lessons covering drugs and alcohol than on, for example, smoking, the proportion doing so has also almost doubled since the late 1980s.

(Figure 13.1, Table 13.1)

On the whole, similar proportions of boys and of girls said that they recalled lessons on the various topics, except that boys were more likely to remember having had lessons on AIDS and on dental health, and girls more likely to remember having had lessons on healthy eating and the risks associated with exposure to the sun.

Older pupils were more likely than younger pupils to have received lessons on most topics, the exceptions being healthy eating and dental health - which were more likely to be remembered by younger pupils - and exercise, and the risks of sunbathing and sunburn, which were reported by similar proportions of pupils in each school year. The proportion of pupils who remembered having lessons about AIDS doubled from 24% in year 9 to 49% in year 10, and given

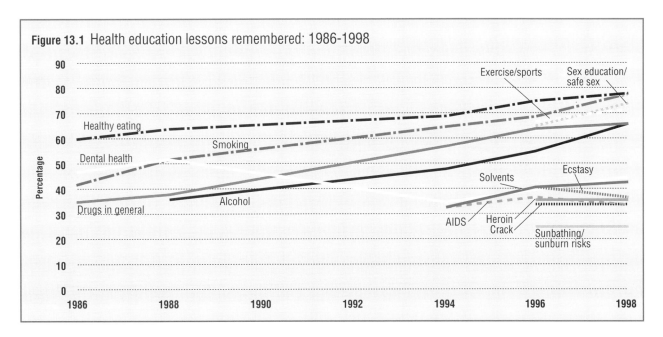

Figure 13.1 Health education lessons remembered: 1986-1998

that they were asked about lessons in the previous year, this suggests that many schools may not tackle this subject until pupils are in year 9. There were similar increases between year 8 and year 9 in the proportions saying they remembered lessons on drugs and alcohol, and also, to a lesser extent, smoking.

(Figure 13.2, Tables 13.2-13.3)

13.3 The association between health education and behaviour

There is occasional discussion in the media as to whether warning children about the risks of, for example, drug taking, might encourage experimentation rather than the reverse. If that were the case, then this survey might expect to find a higher prevalence of smoking among those who remembered having health education lessons about it, and similar associations for drinking and drug use with having had health education on those topics.

It was noted above that remembered exposure to health education on smoking, drinking and drugs increased with progress through the school. Since smoking, drinking and drug use themselves are all more prevalent among older pupils, it is important to take account of this when looking at the association between health education and behaviour.

Overall, for both boys and girls, the proportion who were regular smokers was virtually the same,

regardless of whether or not they remembered having had health education on smoking. When different school years are considered, there is no consistent pattern: among boys in year 11, prevalence was significantly higher among those who remembered having health education on smoking than among those who did not, but among girls of the same age, the opposite was the case.

Similarly, although pupils who remembered having health education about alcohol in the last year were a little more likely than those who had not to be frequent drinkers, this association was not evident in the different school years. This suggests that the overall difference occurred because those who had health education were, on average, older than those who had not, and for that reason also more likely to be drinkers.

In relation to drug use, again, the figures for all pupils suggest slightly higher proportions of drug users among those who had received health education on drugs than among those who had not, but this is once more due to those who had been given education on drugs being older, on average, than those who had not. In most school years the difference was in the opposite direction. Thus, for example, among those in year 10 who remembered having had health education on drugs, 20% of boys and 17% of girls had used drugs at least once, whereas among those with no recollection of drugs education the equivalent figures were 24% and 22% respectively.

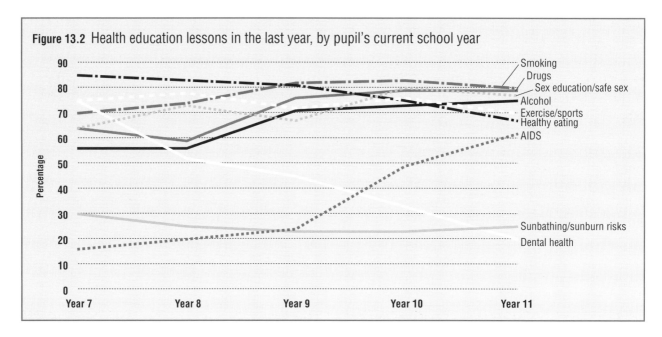

Figure 13.2 Health education lessons in the last year, by pupil's current school year

This is of necessity a somewhat simplistic analysis of the relationship between health education and behaviour in this age group. Although there is no evidence from this survey to suggest that health education encourages the behaviours it is seeking to advise against, there is also none showing that, on the whole, those who remember receiving health education on particular topics are taking the advice given.

(Tables 13.4-13.6)

13.4 **Schools' smoking policies**

In Chapter 1 it was noted that in 1998, in addition to this survey, Social Survey Division also carried out a similar survey in England among 11-15 year olds for the Health Education Authority. On both surveys, the opportunity was taken of asking each co-operating school how smoking on the school premises was dealt with. Of the initial sample of 376 schools selected for the two surveys, 277 took part in the main surveys, and 247 schools[1] provided information for this part of the study. The sample of schools is too small to permit reliable analysis by factors such as type of school, or region, so data are given in the text, and no separate tables included.

A member of the school staff was asked whether the school had a smoking policy for staff and visitors and, if it did, was asked to give some information about it. The staff member was also asked what action was recommended by the policy if pupils were caught smoking on school premises.

Smoking policies for adults

All schools forbid smoking by pupils anywhere on school premises, but this blanket prohibition does not necessarily extend to teachers and other adults.

Nine in ten schools said they had a smoking policy covering staff and visitors to the school. Responsibility for deciding what the policy should be was most likely to be with head teachers and/or school governors: they were involved in 70% and 55% respectively of schools that had policies. Staff participated in the decision in only 22% of schools.

Smoking policies varied in permissiveness: 37% of schools allowed no smoking anywhere on the school premises, including outside in the grounds, and a further 13% permitted smoking outside only. However, the highest proportion, half of those with a policy (45% of all schools) allowed smoking in some areas inside the school building. In most cases this was in specially designated smoking rooms, but about 10% of all schools permitted smoking in the staffroom.

Almost four in five schools said that smoking was prohibited in front of pupils during school hours, but only two thirds said that the smoking policy applied at all times, and not just during school hours.

Smoking among pupils: action taken by the school

The most common action taken if a pupil was found smoking was that the school sent a letter to the child's parents - this happened in about three quarters of all schools - and the two next most common were a warning, given to the offender in two thirds of schools, and a note on his or her record, which happened in about half of all schools.

About one school in ten said they might refer a pupil caught smoking for counselling or help in giving up smoking, and in about one third of schools, suspension or exclusion was considered for repeat offenders.

References

1   The overall response rate of 66% is only approximate, since schools were selected with probability proportional to their size, rather than with equal probability. The data discussed have been re-weighted to take account of the different probabilities of selection.

Table 13.1 Proportion of pupils who remembered receiving health education on various topics in the last year: 1986, 1988, 1994, 1996 and 1998

All pupils *England*

Health education lessons	1986	1988	1994	1996	1998
	%	%	%	%	%
Smoking	42	52	65	69	78
Alcohol+	..	36	48	55	66
Drugs in general+	35	38	57	64	66
Heroin	..	..	..	36	36
Crack	..	..	..	34	34
Ecstasy	..	..	..	41	37
Solvents	..	..	33	41	43
Sex education/safe sex	..	..	..	67	72
AIDS	..	..	33	37	34
Sunbathing/sunburn risks	..	..	..	25	25
Healthy eating	60	74	69	75	78
Dental health	47	52	35	40	45
Exercise/sports	..	..	..	65	74
Bases(=100%)	3189	2759	2971	2705	4328

+ drugs and alcohol were a combined answer category in 1986

Table 13.2 Health education lessons in the last year, by sex

All pupils *England 1998*

Health education lessons	Boys	Girls	Total
	%	%	%
Smoking	78	78	78
Alcohol	66	66	66
Drugs:			
Heroin	37	35	36
Crack	32	30	31
Ecstasy	38 }72	36 }70	37 }71
Solvents	44	42	43
Drugs in general	67	65	66
Sex education/safe sex	71	73	72
AIDS	36	32	34
Sunbathing/sunburn risks	48	52	25
Healthy eating	76	81	78
Dental health	47	43	45
Exercise/sports	74	74	74
Bases(=100%)	872	821	4328

Table 13.3 Health education lessons in the last year, by pupil's current school year

All pupils *England 1998*

Health education lessons Pupil's current school year	Year 7	Year 8	Year 9	Year 10	Year 11	Total
%	%	%	%	%	%	
Smoking	70	74	82	83	80	78
Alcohol	56	56	71	73	75	66
Drugs:						
Heroin	28	24	37	47	46	36
Crack	18	19	33	44	42	31
Ecstasy	26 }64	20 }59	38 }76	51 }79	53 }79	37 }71
Solvents	36	32	46	52	52	43
Drugs in general	56	52	71	75	77	66
Sex education/safe sex	64	73	67	80	77	72
AIDS	16	20	24	49	62	34
Sunbathing/sunburn risks	30	25	23	23	25	25
Healthy eating	85	83	81	75	67	78
Dental health	75	52	45	33	20	45
Exercise/sports	75	78	72	76	70	74
Bases(=100%)	601	666	645	1266	1188	4366

Table 13.4 Smoking behaviour, by sex, school year, and whether remembered having health education lessons on smoking in the last year

All pupils   *England 1998*

| School year | Boys | | | Girls | | | Total | | |
	Yes	No	Total	Yes	No	Total	Yes	No	Total
					% who were regular smokers				
Year 7	0	4	1	0	2	1	0	3	1
Year 8	2	4	3	3	2	3	3	4	3
Year 9	3	13	5	10	7	9	7	10	7
Year 10	16	16	16	21	23	21	19	20	19
Year 11	20	16	19	26	40	29	23	28	24
Total	9	10	9	12	12	12	10	11	10
Bases(=100%)									
Year 7	*216*	*84*	*300*	*224*	*101*	*325*	*439*	*185*	*624*
Year 8	*245*	*95*	*340*	*276*	*86*	*362*	*521*	*182*	*703*
Year 9	*233*	*56*	*289*	*314*	*62*	*376*	*548*	*118*	*666*
Year 10	*548*	*89*	*637*	*539*	*129*	*668*	*1086*	*218*	*1304*
Year 11	*486*	*134*	*620*	*477*	*112*	*589*	*963*	*246*	*1209*
Total	*1690*	*485*	*2175*	*1802*	*503*	*2305*	*3493*	*988*	*4481*

Table 13.5 Usual drinking frequency, by sex, school year, and whether remembered having health education lessons on alcohol in the last year

All pupils   *England 1998*

| School year | Boys | | | Girls | | | Total | | |
	Yes	No	Total	Yes	No	Total	Yes	No	Total
					% who usually drank at least once a week				
Year 7	4	3	4	1	0	0	2	1	2
Year 8	7	8	7	5	5	5	6	7	6
Year 9	9	12	9	10	8	9	9	9	9
Year 10	26	23	25	25	27	25	26	24	25
Year 11	43	48	44	33	33	33	38	41	39
Total	19	16	18	16	11	14	17	14	16
Bases(=100%)									
Year 7	*163*	*127*	*290*	*170*	*133*	*303*	*332*	*259*	*591*
Year 8	*174*	*147*	*321*	*200*	*147*	*347*	*374*	*293*	*667*
Year 9	*209*	*73*	*282*	*250*	*112*	*362*	*459*	*185*	*644*
Year 10	*464*	*157*	*621*	*467*	*182*	*649*	*931*	*339*	*1270*
Year 11	*451*	*159*	*610*	*438*	*143*	*581*	*890*	*302*	*1192*
Total	*1400*	*704*	*2104*	*1461*	*756*	*2217*	*2861*	*1460*	*4321*

Table 13.6 Drug use, by sex, school year, and whether remembered having health education lessons on drugs in the last year

All pupils   *England 1998*

| School year | Boys | | | Girls | | | Total | | |
	Yes	No	Total	Yes	No	Total	Yes	No	Total
					% who had used drugs				
Year 7	2	1	1	1	2	1	1	1	1
Year 8	3	4	4	6	2	4	4	3	4
Year 9	7	20	10	8	13	9	7	16	10
Year 10	20	24	21	17	22	18	19	22	20
Year 11	35	36	35	30	35	31	33	35	33
Total	15	13	14	13	12	12	14	12	13
Bases(=100%)									
Year 7	*195*	*105*	*300*	*206*	*113*	*319*	*401*	*218*	*619*
Year 8	*196*	*128*	*324*	*197*	*149*	*346*	*393*	*277*	*670*
Year 9	*221*	*69*	*290*	*277*	*92*	*369*	*497*	*161*	*658*
Year 10	*510*	*120*	*630*	*509*	*152*	*661*	*1020*	*274*	*1294*
Year 11	*504*	*122*	*626*	*454*	*134*	*588*	*958*	*256*	*1214*
Total	*1560*	*591*	*2151*	*1585*	*680*	*2265*	*3146*	*1270*	*4416*

14 Comparison of smoking, drinking and drug use in England and Scotland

14.1 **Introduction**

The comparison of results for England with those for Scotland should be treated with caution: since the education system is different in the two countries, the populations covered by the surveys are not quite the same. In Scotland, pupils transfer to secondary school a year later than in England, and transfer is usually based on the child's age on 1 March, rather than at the beginning of the school year. Because of these factors, only 7% of the sample in Scotland are aged 11, (and they are combined in analysis with

12 year olds): in England, 17% of the sample were aged 11. At the other end of the age range, there were virtually no 16 year olds in the sample in Scotland, but 3% of the sample in England were aged 16 (and are combined in analysis with 15 year olds). The net result is that, on average, the sample in Scotland is about six weeks older than the sample in England.

Since smoking, drinking and drug use all increase with age, the difference in age structure of the two samples should be borne in mind when interpreting differences between the two countries.

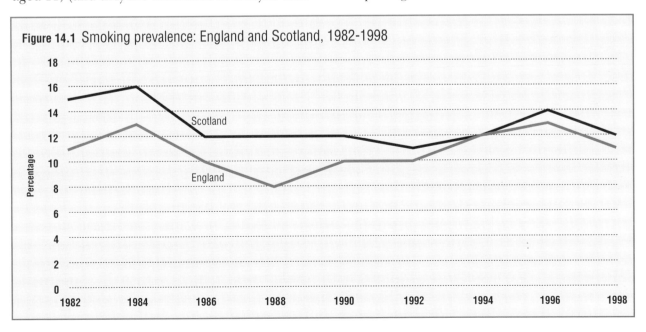

Figure 14.1 Smoking prevalence: England and Scotland, 1982-1998

14.2 Smoking

Throughout the series of surveys, the prevalence of smoking has consistently been higher in Scotland than in England, although in recent years the difference has narrowed and has not been great enough to be statistically significant. In 1998, 11% of 11-15 year olds in England, and 12% of 12-15 year olds in Scotland were regular smokers (smoking at least one cigarette a week). Around three quarters of regular smokers in both countries said that they would find it difficult to give up smoking, and similar proportions said that they had tried to give up.

Current smokers in Scotland – and, in particular, girls – were more likely than those in England to keep their smoking secret from their families, or at least, to think that their families didn't know about it. In Scotland, 49% of boys and as many as 65% of girls said that their family (by which they probably meant their parents) did not know they smoked. The equivalent figures for England were 40% and 47% respectively.

(Figure 14.1, Tables 14.1-14.3)

14.3 Where children get cigarettes

Pupils in Scotland were more likely than those in England to have tried to buy cigarettes sometime during the last year (30% compared with 22%), and they were a little less likely to have been refused at least once, although the difference was not large enough to be statistically significant.

Not all children who buy cigarettes are getting them for themselves, and the higher proportion trying to buy cigarettes in Scotland may be accounted for by the fact that pupils who bought cigarettes last time were twice as likely as those in England to say they had bought them for their mother or father. It is, nonetheless, illegal to sell cigarettes to children under 16, whoever they say they are for.

The usual sources of cigarettes for current smokers were similar in the two countries, but the proportions of smokers saying they obtained cigarettes from garage shops, vending machines and from friends or relatives were higher in England than in Scotland.

(Tables 14.4-14.6)

14.4 Drinking in the previous week

Throughout the series of surveys, the proportion of pupils who drank alcohol during the week before the survey has been lower in Scotland than in England, and this remained the case in 1998. Average consumption per pupil was slightly lower in Scotland than in England (1.4, compared with 1.6 units), but the average amount drunk by those who did drink was similar in the two countries. In both England and Scotland, boys were more likely than girls to have drunk alcohol in the previous week, and they drank more than girls.

Until 1998, alcohol consumption appeared to be increasing in both countries. It is not clear

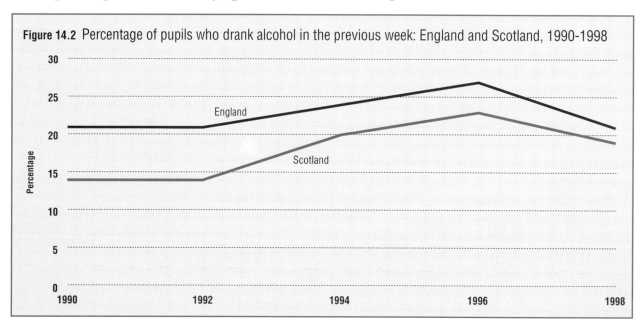

Figure 14.2 Percentage of pupils who drank alcohol in the previous week: England and Scotland, 1990-1998

whether the slight downturn in 1998 is the start of a new trend, or a short term fluctuation.

The proportion of all pupils who had drunk each type of drink was similar in the two countries, except that Scottish pupils were less likely to have drunk beer, lager or cider (11% of pupils in Scotland, compared with 14% in England). When the analysis is restricted to those who had drunk alcohol in the previous week, as well as being comparatively less likely to have drunk beer, lager and cider, those in Scotland were more likely to have drunk spirits and alcopops than were drinkers in England.

(Figure 14.2, Table 14.7)

14.5 **Usual drinking behaviour**

It was noted above that pupils in Scotland were less likely than those in England to have had a drink in the previous week, and as would be expected, they were also a little less likely to say that they usually drank at least once a week – 14% of those in Scotland, compared with 16% of those in England, did so.

There were marked differences in where children drank and who they were usually with: compared with those in England, pupils in Scotland were less likely to drink at home, at parties, or in a pub or bar, and much more likely to say they usually drank somewhere else – probably indicating that they drank out of doors. Those in Scotland were also comparatively more

likely to drink with friends, and less likely to drink with their parents: 44% of English drinkers said they usually drank with their parents, compared with only 31% of Scottish drinkers.

A sizeable proportion of drinkers in both countries – 53% in England and 47% in Scotland – said that they never bought alcohol. Among those who did buy alcohol, off-licences were the most common place of purchase in both countries.

(Table 14.8)

14.6 **Drug use**

Pupils in Scotland were more likely than those in England to have been offered drugs – in Scotland, 41% had been offered at least one of the drugs on the list they were shown, compared with 34% in England. They were also more likely to have tried drugs: 18% of pupils in Scotland had used drugs, but only 13% of pupils in England had done so.

These overall differences were reflected to varying degrees in the proportions who had been offered individual drugs. The most marked differences between the two countries were in relation to cannabis (34% of pupils in Scotland had been offered cannabis, compared with 26% in England) psychedelic drugs (14% in Scotland had been offered LSD or magic mushrooms, compared with 8% in England), and glue (13% compared with 8%). The only drugs which were

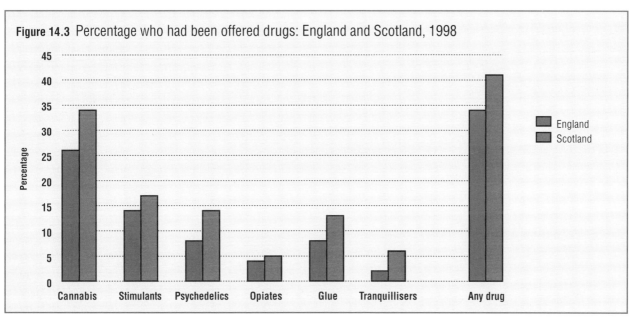

Figure 14.3 Percentage who had been offered drugs: England and Scotland, 1998

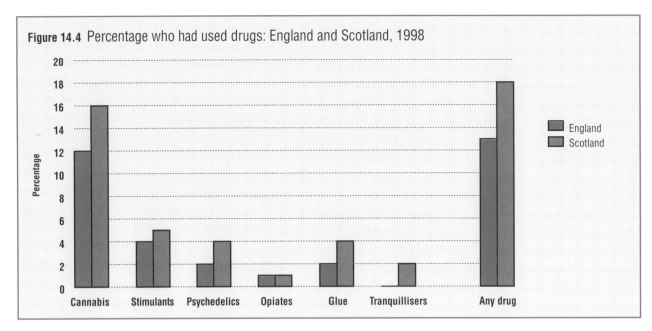

Figure 14.4 Percentage who had used drugs: England and Scotland, 1998

not significantly more likely to have been offered to pupils in Scotland than to those in England were cocaine, crack, poppers, opiates and steroids.

Differences between the two countries in the proportions who had used particular drugs were similar, albeit at a lower level: 16% of pupils in Scotland had used cannabis, compared with 12% of pupils in England, and pupils in Scotland were twice as likely to have used psychedelic drugs and glue (in both cases, 4% of pupils in Scotland had done so, compared with 2% of pupils in England).

(Figures 14.3-14.4, Tables 14.9-14.10)

Table 14.1
Prevalence of smoking by sex: England and Scotland 1982 to 1998

All pupils

Survey year*	England			Scotland		
	Boys	Girls	Total	Boys	Girls	Total
1982	11	11	11	15	14	15
1984	13	13	13	16	17	16
1986	7	12	10	10	14	12
1988	7	9	8	..	..	..
1990	9	11	10	11	12	12
1992	9	10	10	10	13	11
1994	10	13	12	11	13	12
1996	11	15	13	14	14	14
1998	9	12	11	11	13	12
1998 base (=100%)	*2311*	*2413*	*4723*	*1743*	*1780*	*3526*

* The survey was not carried out in Scotland in 1988

Table 14.2 Perceived dependence on cigarettes: England and Scotland, 1998

Regular smokers

Perceived dependence	England (age 11-15)			Scotland (age 12-15)		
	Boys	Girls	Total	Boys	Girls	Total
Would find it difficult not to smoke for a week	54	60	58	64	61	63
Would find it difficult to give up altogether	67	74	72	76	74	75
Would like to give up altogether	38	32	35	40	42	41
Has tried to give up	69	74	72	72	79	76
Base (=100%)	*199*	*277*	*476*	*185*	*227*	*412*

Table 14.3 Attitude of the smoker's family: England and Scotland, 1998

Current smokers

Attitude of family	England (age 11-15)			Scotland (age 12-15)		
	Boys	Girls	Total	Boys	Girls	Total
Family:						
try to stop me	6	5	5	7	4	5
persuade me not to	31	30	30	26	21	23
don't mind	12	11	11	12	6	9
Don't know	11	7	9	5	4	4
They don't know I smoke	40	47	44	49	65	58
Base (=100%)	*311*	*409*	*720*	*264*	*371*	*635*

Table 14.4 Purchase of cigarettes: England and Scotland, 1998

	England (age 11-15)			Scotland (age 12-15)		
	Boys	Girls	Total	Boys	Girls	Total
% of all pupils who tried to buy cigarettes in the last year	20	23	22	25	34	30
% of those who tried to buy who were refused at least once	44	42	43	40	41	40
% of all pupils who tried to buy and were refused at least once	8	10	9	10	14	12
Bases(=100%)						
All pupils	*2330*	*2411*	*4741*	*1743*	*1789*	*3532*
Those who tried to buy	*442*	*539*	*981*	*434*	*606*	*1040*

Table 14.5 Who the cigarettes were for last time: England and Scotland, 1998

Who the cigarettes were for	England	Scotland
% who were successful last time	86	86
Who the cigarettes were for:		
Self	52	42
Mother	7	15
Father	4	6
A friend	34	33
Brother or sister	3	3
Someone else	12	15
Bases (=100%)		
All who were successful last time	*846*	*893*
All who tried to buy in the last year	*982*	*1042*

Table 14.6 Usual source of cigarettes: England and Scotland, 1998

Current smokers

Usual source of cigarettes	England	Scotland
Bought from newsagents/ tobacconist/sweet shop	65	62
Bought from garage shop	35	27
Bought from supermarket	19	16
Bought from other type of shop	16	17
Bought from machine	24	19
Bought from friends/relatives	28	23
Bought from someone else	16	15
Given by friends	61	60
Given by brother/sister	16	13
Given by mother/father	8	5
Found or taken	7	8
Base (=100%)		
Current smokers	*727*	*640*
% of current smokers who usually bought cigarettes from a shop who found it easy to do so		
Boys	74	77
Girls	82	86
All current smokers	78	82
Bases (=100%)		
Current smokers who had bought from a shop	*594*	*516*

Table 14.7 Drinking last week: England and Scotland

| | England (age 11-15) | | | | | 1998 | | Scotland (age 12-15) | | | | | 1998 |
	1990	1992	1994	1996	1998	base		1990	1992	1994	1996	1998	base
% who drank last week													
Boys	22	24	26	27	23	2249		16	16	21	24	20	1715
Girls	20	17	22	26	18	2362		12	13	19	21	17	1776
Total	21	21	24	27	21	4609		14	14	20	23	19	3494
Average units drunk last week per pupil													
Boys	0.9	1.4	1.5	2.1	1.9	2093		1.0	1.1	1.6	2.2	1.8	1605
Girls	0.7	0.7	1.0	1.5	1.2	2273		0.5	0.7	1.0	1.6	1.0	1697
Total	0.8	1.1	1.3	1.8	1.6	4367		0.8	0.9	1.3	1.9	1.4	3301
Percentage of pupils who had drunk each type of drink													
Beer, lager, cider	14	16	18	19	14			9	10	14	14	11	
Shandy	6	5	6	5	4			3	4	3	4	2	
Wine	10	11	11	10	10			6	7	10	11	8	
Fortified wine	4	4	3	4	4			3	3	4	3	3	
Spirits	7	8	9	12	10			6	7	11	13	11	
Alcopops	..	..	..	14	7			..	..	..	12	8	
Average units drunk last week per drinker													
Boys	6.0	7.0	7.4	9.7	11.3	351		10.3	9.1	10.6	11.9	12.8	228
Girls	4.8	4.7	5.4	7.0	8.4	334		6.0	6.9	6.9	10.0	7.8	224
Total	5.4	6.0	6.4	8.4	9.9	686		8.4	8.2	8.7	11.1	10.3	452
Percentage of drinkers who had drunk each type of drink													
Beer, lager, cider	67	76	76	74	71			65	73	70	67	62	
Shandy	31	25	24	20	18			24	25	16	21	13	
Wine	50	52	48	40	51			47	49	51	51	49	
Martini, sherry	18	17	15	15	20			19	20	20	15	18	
Spirits, liqueurs	35	37	39	45	54			46	50	60	61	65	
Alcopops	..	..	..	55	37			..	..	..	57	44	

Table 14.8 Usual drinking behaviour: England and Scotland, 1998

| | England (age 11-15) | | | Scotland (age 12-15) | | |
	Boys	Girls	Total	Boys	Girls	Total
Usual drinking frequency						
At least once a week	18	14	16	15	13	14
Less than once a week	39	40	40	41	41	41
Doesn't drink at all	43	46	44	44	46	45
Where usually drinks						
Pub or bar	12	12	12	4	5	4
Club or disco	10	11	10	9	11	10
Parties with friends	23	24	23	18	18	18
At home, or someone else's home	60	56	58	47	50	48
Somewhere else	22	21	21	41	39	40
Who usually drinks with						
Boy/girlfriend	6	8	7	5	6	6
Friends of same sex	19	16	18	22	15	19
Friends of opposite sex	4	4	4	4	3	4
Friends of both sexes	32	39	36	41	51	46
Parents	46	43	44	30	32	31
Brothers or sisters	16	16	16	15	11	13
Alone	5	2	3	3	1	2
Where usually buys alcohol						
Pub or bar	9	9	9	4	3	3
Club or disco	6	6	6	3	2	3
Off-licence	22	18	20	20	17	18
Shop or supermarket	11	10	10	14	13	14
From a friend or relative	10	9	9	11	13	12
Somewhere else	7	6	6	12	13	13
Never buys alcohol	51	56	53	47	47	47
Bases (=100%)						
Those who drink	1411	1397	2808	1095	1079	2174

Table 14.9 Drug use: England and Scotland, 1998

	England (age 11-15)			Scotland (age 12-15)		
	Boys	Girls	Total	Boys	Girls	Total
% who had been offered drugs						
11 years	18	12	15	..	..	..
12 years	22	16	19	24	18	21
13 years	33	28	30	40	35	38
14 years	45	44	44	56	50	53
15 years	61	61	61	70	66	68
All ages	36	32	34	44	38	41
% who had used drugs						
11 years	1	1	1	..	..	..
12 years	4	4	5	3	4	3
13 years	10	9	9	16	11	13
14 years	18	16	18	27	23	25
15 years	33	30	31	41	38	39
All ages	14	12	13	19	16	18
Base (=100%)						
11 years	*305*	*305*	*610*	*..*	*..*	*..*
12 years	*353*	*373*	*727*	*387*	*393*	*780*
13 years	*303*	*388*	*692*	*373*	*392*	*765*
14 years	*610*	*671*	*1282*	*559*	*606*	*1165*
15 years	*756*	*674*	*1430*	*425*	*403*	*828*
All ages	*2327*	*2411*	*4741*	*1744*	*1794*	*3538*

Table 14.10 Whether had been offered individual drugs, by sex

All pupils

Type of drug	% who had been offered the drug		% who had used the drug	
	England	Scotland	England	Scotland
Cannabis	26	34	12	16
Stimulants				
Cocaine	6 ⎫	6 ⎫	1 ⎫	1 ⎫
Crack	3 ⎪	3 ⎪	0 ⎪	0 ⎪
Ecstasy	6 ⎬ 14	9 ⎬ 17	1 ⎬ 4	1 ⎬ 5
Amphetamines	7 ⎪	11 ⎪	3 ⎪	4 ⎪
Poppers	6 ⎭	6 ⎭	2 ⎭	2 ⎭
Psychedelics				
LSD	6 ⎫ 8	9 ⎫ 14	1 ⎫ 2	2 ⎫ 4
Magic Mushrooms	6 ⎭	10 ⎭	2 ⎭	3 ⎭
Opiates				
Heroin	4 ⎫ 4	5 ⎫ 5	0 ⎫ 1	1 ⎫ 1
Methadone	1 ⎭	2 ⎭	0 ⎭	0 ⎭
Glue	8	13	2	4
Tranquilisers	2	6	0	2
Steroids	2	2	0	0
Semeron	1	2	0	0
Other drugs	6	6	1	2
Base (=100%)	*4751*	*4649*	*3540*	*3530*

Appendix A: **The sample**

A sample was required of children of secondary school age with separate national samples for England and Scotland. The sample for Scotland is described in the separate survey report for Scotland.[1]

In England the target population was children who were in years 7 to 11 inclusive in secondary schools or at an equivalent level in middle and upper schools.

The survey covered almost all types of secondary school (comprehensive, secondary modern, grammar, technical, and other secondary schools) in both the maintained and non-maintained sectors of education. Only pupils attending special schools (for children with learning disabilities) and hospital special schools (for children spending a period in hospital) were excluded from the survey.

The sample was selected in two stages. At the first stage a sample of schools was selected from a list of all schools in England taken from the 1998 school database supplied by the School's Register for the Department for Education and Employment. At the second stage an interviewer visited each selected school and drew a sample of pupils from school registers.

Probabilities of selection

Given the requirement that each child in the target population should have the same probability of being selected to take part in the survey, the overall probability of selection, or sampling fraction, is the product of the sampling fractions at the first and second stages, i.e.

$$F = f_1 \times f_2$$

where f_1 = probability of selecting the school
f_2 = probability of selecting the pupil

Schools with probability proportional to the number of pupils aged 11-15, so that roughly equal numbers of pupils could be sampled from each selected school. Thus :

$$f_1 = n_1 \times \frac{s}{S}$$

where n_1 = total number of schools to be selected
s = number of pupils in an individual school aged 11-15
S = total number of pupils aged 11-15

and $F = \dfrac{n_2}{S}$

where n_2 = number of pupils to be selected from each school

Overall, therefore, for each pupil the sampling fraction is:

$$F = (n_1 \times \frac{s}{S}) \times (\frac{n_2}{S}) = \frac{n_1 \times n_2}{S}$$

Sample size

The survey aimed to achieve a sample of about 5,000 pupils in England. To achieve this a sample of 200 schools was drawn in England. Based on experience, it was expected that about 90% of schools would co-operate, and assuming that 90% of selected pupils would agree to take part in the survey, the average size of quota selected in each co-operating school to achieve the required sample size would be about 30 pupils.

As in previous years, schools with fewer than 35 pupils in the required age ranges were deleted from the sampling frame.

Stratification of the sampling frame

Previous surveys in the series have shown that children's behaviour varies according to the characteristics of the school rather more than by region, so schools were stratified in England as follows :

1.   Into three school types:
      LEA maintained
      Grant maintained
      Independent

2.   Then, by selection policy into:
      comprehensive
      selective
      secondary modern
      (except for Independent schools which were separated into selective and non-selective)

3. Finally the larger strata were split into :
    boys only
    girls only
    mixed

4. In each of the 16 major strata formed, schools were ordered by local education authority within region.

Tables A1 shows the allocation of the required sample of schools to each of the major strata and the number of schools actually selected in England.

(Table A1)

Sampling within selected schools

To provide better estimates of smoking, drinking, and drug use among the target age group, the sample size was increased in 1998 by oversampling older pupils, among whom prevalence of smoking, alcohol and drug use are relatively high: those in school years 10 and 11 were oversampled by a factor of 2.

Sampling fractions at the second stage (i.e. within schools) were calculated in the office and adjusted to compensate for the effect of rounding on the number of schools selected in each stratum at the first stage. Expected quota sizes are shown in Table A2. These were based on information about the number of pupils at each school collected in the previous six months, and actual quota sizes therefore varied to the extent to which the size of the school had changed in the interim.

(Table A2)

Sampling at each co-operating school was carried out by an ONS interviewer. The instructions to which the interviewers worked were the same as in previous surveys.

Precision of results and the measurement of change

Since the data in this report were obtained from a sample of the population, they are subject to sampling error. Any sample is only one of an almost infinite number that might have been selected, all producing slightly different estimates. Sampling error stems from the probability that any selected sample is not completely representative of the population from which it is drawn.

Sampling error shows the amount by which the value of a sample estimate of a variable can be expected to differ from the true value of that variable in the population. With a simple random sample, the formula for calculating the sampling error for a percentage p, is :

$$\sqrt{\frac{p\,(100-p)}{n}}$$

where n is the sample size.

Since the sample of pupils was clustered in schools, sampling errors are not the same as they would have been for a simple random sample of the same size. Sampling errors for four key variables which take account of the complex design are shown later on in this chapter.

The formula for calculating sampling errors of differences in percentages between surveys assuming simple random samples is :

$$\sqrt{\frac{p_1\,(100-p_1)}{n_1} + \frac{p_2\,(100-p_2)}{n_1}}$$

In general, attention is drawn to differences between estimates only when they are significant at the 0.05 confidence level, thus indicating that there is less than a 5% probability that the observed difference is due to random sampling variation and that no difference occurred in the population from which the sample is drawn.

It is important to recognise that sampling error is only one of the sources of error which affect the accuracy of any survey results. Other sources of inaccuracy include non-response bias, and over- and under-reporting, both of which are difficult to quantify. It can be assumed, however, that since the results compared in this report are from surveys conducted in the same way and using the same methods of collecting information, non-sampling errors will be similar on each survey and so will not affect comparisons.

Sampling errors

Tables A3-A6 give true standard errors and 95% confidence intervals, taking account of the complex sample design and the weighted sample, for four key variables. Since the survey used a multi-stage sample design which involved both clustering and stratification it is not appropriate to calculate standard errors using the formulae which assumes a simple random sample design.[2] Only a few of the key estimates are presented because of the large number of possible estimates which could be covered. The standard errors of other survey variables can be estimated by using the formula which assumes a simple random sample and applying a design factor of 1.1.

(Tables A3-A5)

References

1. Goddard E and Higgins V. *Smoking, drinking and drug use among young teenagers in 1998: Scotland,* 1999 (London: SO)

2. The calculation of the standard errors and design factors presented uses the package STATA. For further details of the method of calculation see Butcher B and Elliot D. *A sampling errors manual,* 1987 (London :OPCS)

Table A1 Allocation of primary sampling units to strata

England 1998

Type of school		Population	Estimated PSUs	Actual PSUs
Secondary schools				
LEA comprehensive				
Boys		53508	3.71	4
Girls		90379	6.26	6
Mixed		1799940	124.70	125
LEA selective	All	40445	2.80	3
LEA modern	Single sex	16068	1.10	1
Mixed		53952	3.74	4
GM comprehensive				
Boys		29084	2.01	2
Girls		25201	1.75	2
Mixed		372237	25.79	26
GM selective	All	62549	4.33	4
GM modern	All	31353	2.17	2
Independent selective				
Boys		46663	3.23	3
Girls		57031	3.95	4
Mixed		75890	5.26	5
Independent non-selective				
	All	38480	2.67	3
Middle schools				
Middle deemed primary		14599	1.01	1
Middle deemed secondary		79513	5.51	5
Total		2886892	200.00	200

Table A2 Quota sizes and maximum sample sizes expected, by school type

England 1998

Type of school		Sampled schools	Quota size	Maximum sample
Secondary schools				
LEA comprehensive				
Boys		4	31	124
Girls		6	35	210
Mixed		125	33	4125
LEA selective	All	3	31	93
LEA modern				
	Single sex	1	37	37
	Mixed	4	31	124
GM comprehensive				
Boys		2	33	66
Girls		2	29	58
Mixed		26	33	858
GM selective	All	4	36	144
GM modern	All	2	36	72
Independent selective				
Boys		3	36	108
Girls		4	33	132
Mixed		5	35	175
Independent non-selective				
	All	3	29	87
Middle schools				
Middle deemed primary		1	33	33
Middle deemed secondary		5	36	180
Total		200		6626

Table A3 True standard errors and 95% confidence intervals for the prevalence of smoking, by sex and age

England 1998

	Sample size	%(p)	True standard error of p	95% confidence interval lower	95% confidence interval upper	Deft
Boys						
Age 11	263	1.05%	0.62%	0.00%	2.27%	0.99
Age 12	315	3.09%	1.02%	1.08%	5.10%	1.05
Age 13	259	5.08%	1.14%	2.84%	7.32%	0.84
Age 14	686	14.92%	1.39%	12.20%	17.65%	1.02
Age 15	841	19.08%	1.36%	16.42%	21.75%	1.00
Total	2358	9.09%	0.65%	7.80%	10.37%	1.10
Girls						
Age 11	266	0.98%	0.72%	0.00%	2.40%	1.20
Age 12	315	2.70%	1.05%	0.63%	4.76%	1.15
Age 13	305	8.93%	1.62%	5.76%	12.10%	0.99
Age 14	723	19.21%	1.53%	16.21%	22.20%	1.04
Age 15	756	29.29%	1.61%	26.13%	32.44%	0.97
Total	2367	12.24%	0.73%	10.82%	13.67%	1.08
Total						
Age 11	529	1.02%	0.48%	0.08%	1.95%	1.09
Age 12	630	2.89%	0.75%	1.42%	4.36%	1.12
Age 13	564	7.23%	1.07%	5.14%	9.32%	0.98
Age 14	1409	17.15%	1.06%	15.07%	19.24%	1.06
Age 15	1597	23.83%	0.98%	21.92%	25.75%	0.92
Total	4725	10.70%	0.52%	9.69%	11.71%	1.15

Table A4 True standard errors and 95% confidence intervals for the proportion who usually drink at least once a week, by sex and age

England 1998

	Sample size	%(p)	True standard error of p	95% confidence interval lower	upper	Deft
Boys						
Age 11	254	4.12%	1.27%	1.63%	6.60%	1.02
Age 12	295	6.43%	1.45%	3.59%	9.27%	1.02
Age 13	253	9.82%	1.92%	6.05%	13.58%	1.03
Age 14	671	20.99%	1.66%	17.74%	24.25%	1.06
Age 15	828	41.61%	2.01%	37.67%	45.54%	1.17
Total	2301	17.48%	0.91%	15.69%	19.27%	1.15
Girls						
Age 11	256	0.99%	0.59%	-0.16%	2.14%	0.95
Age 12	309	4.58%	1.25%	2.13%	7.02%	1.05
Age 13	298	10.64%	2.05%	6.63%	14.65%	1.14
Age 14	707	20.27%	1.59%	17.15%	23.39%	1.05
Age 15	746	32.56%	1.98%	28.68%	36.43%	1.15
Total	2316	13.85%	0.81%	12.26%	15.44%	1.13
Total						
Age 11	510	2.57%	0.71%	1.19%	3.96%	1.01
Age 12	604	5.48%	1.05%	3.42%	7.55%	1.14
Age 13	551	10.27%	1.41%	7.51%	13.03%	1.09
Age 14	1378	20.62%	1.24%	18.18%	23.05%	1.14
Age 15	1574	37.40%	1.41%	34.64%	40.15%	1.15
Total	4617	15.63%	0.66%	14.34%	16.93%	1.24

Table A5 True standard errors and 95% confidence intervals for mean alcohol consumption last week, by sex and age

England 1998

	Sample size	%(p)	True standard error of p	95% confidence interval lower	upper	Deft
Boys						
Age 11	244	0.05	0.03	0.00	0.12	1.01
Age 12	282	0.38	0.13	0.12	0.63	1.25
Age 13	238	0.74	0.24	0.25	1.22	1.47
Age 14	622	2.59	0.39	1.81	3.36	0.94
Age 15	738	5.22	0.44	4.35	6.10	0.95
Total	2124	1.89	0.15	1.59	2.20	1.06
Girls						
Age 11	255	0.12	0.11	0.00	0.34	1.22
Age 12	302	0.24	0.11	0.21	0.45	1.23
Age 13	289	0.58	0.18	0.21	0.95	1.22
Age 14	669	1.96	0.26	1.45	2.48	1.01
Age 15	698	3.42	0.34	2.73	4.11	0.98
Total	2213	1.24	0.98	1.04	1.44	1.01
Total						
Age 11	499	0.09	0.58	0.00	0.20	1.22
Age 12	584	0.30	0.08	0.14	0.47	1.22
Age 13	527	0.65	0.15	0.34	0.95	1.37
Age 14	1291	2.26	0.21	1.83	2.69	0.89
Age 15	1436	4.36	0.30	3.76	4.95	1.01
Total	4337	1.55	0.94	1.37	1.74	1.10

Table A6 True standard errors and 95% confidence intervals for the proportion who have ever used drugs, by sex and age

England 1998

	Sample size	%(p)	True standard error of p	95% confidence interval lower	upper	Deft
Boys						
Age 11	268	0.88%	0.51%	0.00%	1.88%	0.90
Age 12	309	4.32%	1.13%	2.10%	6.54%	0.98
Age 13	360	9.75%	1.91%	6.02%	13.49%	1.22
Age 14	684	18.44%	1.60%	15.30%	21.58%	1.08
Age 15	845	32.87%	1.58%	29.77%	35.97%	0.98
Total	2466	13.95%	0.74%	12.51%	15.40%	1.06
Girls						
Age 11	168	0.75%	0.53%	0.00%	1.78%	0.79
Age 12	314	4.02%	1.06%	1.94%	6.09%	0.95
Age 13	304	8.59%	1.69%	5.28%	11.89%	1.05
Age 14	724	16.50%	1.40%	13.75%	19.25%	1.02
Age 15	757	29.66%	2.01%	25.72%	33.60%	1.21
Total	2267	11.92%	0.67%	10.61%	13.24%	0.99
Total						
Age 11	436	0.82%	0.36%	0.10%	1.53%	0.85
Age 12	623	4.16%	0.81%	2.59%	5.74%	1.01
Age 13	664	9.10%	1.29%	6.57%	11.64%	1.16
Age 14	1408	17.43%	1.16%	15.16%	19.70%	1.14
Age 15	1602	31.38%	1.13%	29.17%	33.59%	0.97
Total	4733	12.92%	0.49%	11.96%	13.88%	1.00

Appendix B

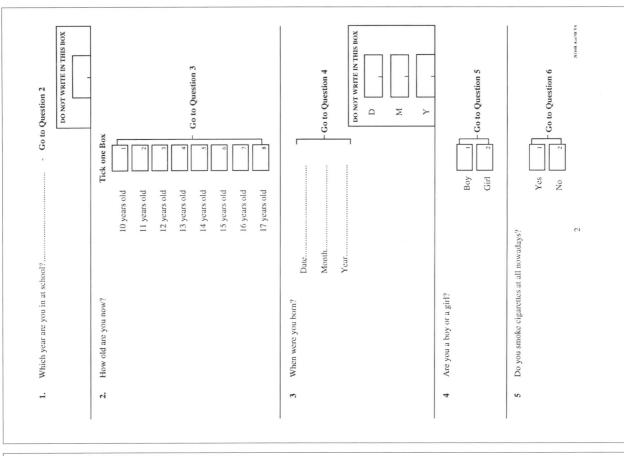

NATIONAL STATISTICS

SURVEY OF SCHOOLCHILDREN SMOKING N1448 - ENGLAND

1998
A

IN CONFIDENCE

STICK SERIAL
NO. LABEL

Most of the questions can be answered by putting a tick in the box next to the answer that applies to you - like this

Yes [✓]₁   No [ ]₂

or sometimes you have to write a number in the box, for example [2]

Some questions don't apply to everybody. It always tells you by the box which question you should answer next.

DO NOT WRITE IN THESE BOXES

Date of interview

DAY	MONTH	YEAR
		9 8

Time of interview

AM	PM
1	2

N1448 Aut98 V4

---

1. Which year are you in at school? .... - Go to Question 2

DO NOT WRITE IN THIS BOX

2. How old are you now?

Tick one Box

10 years old [ ]1
11 years old [ ]2
12 years old [ ]3
13 years old [ ]4
14 years old [ ]5
15 years old [ ]6
16 years old [ ]7
17 years old [ ]8

Go to Question 3

3. When were you born?

Date..............
Month.............
Year.............

Go to Question 4

DO NOT WRITE IN THIS BOX
D
M
Y

4. Are you a boy or a girl?

Boy [ ]1
Girl [ ]2

Go to Question 5

5. Do you smoke cigarettes at all nowadays?

Yes [ ]1
No [ ]2

Go to Question 6

2

N1448 Aut98 V4

9. How long is it since you started smoking at least one cigarette a week?

- Less than 3 months [1]
- 3 - 6 months [2]
- 6 months to 1 year [3]
- more than one year [4]

Go to Question 10

10. How easy or difficult would you find it to go without smoking for as long as a week?

- Very difficult [1]
- Fairly difficult [2]
- Fairly easy [3]
- Very easy [4]

Go to Question 11

11. How easy or difficult would you find it to give up smoking altogether if you wanted to?

- Very difficult [1]
- Fairly difficult [2]
- Fairly easy [3]
- Very easy [4]

Go to Question 12

12. Would you like to give up smoking altogether?

- Yes [1]
- No [2]
- I don't know [3]

Go to Question 13

13. Have you ever tried to give up smoking?

- Yes [1]
- No [2]

Go to Question 14

6. Now read all the following statements carefully and tick the box next to the one which best describes you.

- I have never smoked [1] → Go to Question 7
- I have only ever tried smoking once [2] → Go to Question 8
- I used to smoke sometimes but I never smoke a cigarette now [3] → Go to Question 8
- I sometimes smoke cigarettes now but I don't smoke as many as one a week [4] → Go to Question 14
- I usually smoke between one and six cigarettes a week [5] → Go to Question 9
- I usually smoke more than six cigarettes a week [6] → Go to Question 9

7. Just to check, read the statements below carefully and tick the box next to the one which best describes you.

- I have never tried smoking a cigarette, not even a puff or two [1] → Go to Question 8
- I did once have a puff or two of a cigarette, but I never smoke now [2] → Go to Question 8
- I do sometimes smoke cigarettes [3] → Go to Question 14

8. How do you think your family would feel if you started smoking?

- They would stop me [1]
- They would try to persuade me not to smoke [2]
- They would do nothing [3]
- They would encourage me to smoke [4]
- I don't know [5]

Go to Question 19

14. How does your family feel about you smoking?

They stop me — 1
They try to persuade me not to smoke — 2
They do nothing — 3
They encourage me to smoke — 4
They don't know I smoke — 5
I don't know — 6

Go to Question 15

15. Are you allowed to smoke at home if you want to?

Yes — 1
No — 2
I don't know — 3

Go to Question 16

16. Where do you **usually** get your cigarettes from? (Please tick more than one box if you **often** get cigarettes from different people or places.)

I buy them from a supermarket — 1
I buy them from a newsagent, tobacconist or sweet shop — 2
I buy them from a garage shop — 3
I buy them from some other type of shop — 4
I buy them from a machine — 5
I buy them from friends/relatives — 6
I buy them from someone else — 7
Friends give them to me — 8
My brother or sister gives them to me — 9
My mother or father gives them to me — 10
I take them — 11
I get them in some other way — 12

Go to Question 17

17. On the whole, do you find it easy or difficult to buy cigarettes from a shop?

Very difficult — 1
Fairly difficult — 2
Fairly easy — 3
Very easy — 4
I don't usually buy cigarettes from a shop — 5

Go to Question 18

18. How old were you when you first tried smoking a cigarette, even if it was only a puff or two? Write in the box your **age then**, in numbers, not words.

I was [ ] years old - **Go to Question 19**

19. In the past year, have you ever gone **into a shop** to buy cigarettes? This includes buying cigarettes for somebody else.

Yes — 1 **Go to Question 20**
No — 2 **Go to Question 25**

20. At **any** of these times when you went into a shop to buy cigarettes, did the shopkeeper refuse to sell them to you?

Yes — 1 **Go to Question 21**
No — 2

21. The **last** time you went into a shop to buy cigarettes, what happened?

I bought some cigarettes — 1 **Go to Question 22**
They refused to sell me any cigarettes — 2 **Go to Question 24**

22. How many cigarettes did you buy last time? Write the **number** in the box.

I bought [ ] cigarettes - **Go to Question 23**

23. Did you buy them for yourself or for someone else?

- For myself [1]
- For my mother [2]
- For my father [3]
- For my brother or sister [4]
- For a friend [5]
- For someone else [6]

Go to Question 24

24. How often do you buy cigarettes **from a shop**?

- Almost every day [1]
- Once or twice a week [2]
- Two or three times a month [3]
- About once a month [4]
- Only a few times a year [5]

Go to Question 25

25. How often do you buy cigarettes **from a machine**?

- Almost every day [1]
- Once or twice a week [2]
- Two or three times a month [3]
- About once a month [4]
- Only a few times a year [5]
- Never buy from machine [6]

Go to Question 27

7

N1448 Aut98 V4

---

26. Thinking about the last time you bought cigarettes from a machine, where was the machine situated?

- A pub, club restaurant or somewhere else where alcohol was for sale [1]
- A cafe or restaurant where alcohol was not for sale [2]
- Amusement arcade [3]
- Petrol station [4]
- Somewhere else (**please specify**) [5]

Go to Question 27

27. How much money of your own do you have most weeks to spend as you like?

- Nothing [1] — Go to Question 29
- Less than £1 a week [2]
- £1 or more but less than £5 [3]
- £5 or more but less than £10 [4]
- £10 or more but less than £20 [5]
- £20 or more a week [6] — Go to Question 28

28. Does this money come from —

You may tick more than one box

- pocket money [1]
- paid work outside school hours [2] — Go to Question 29
- or somewhere else? [3]

29. Have you ever had a proper alcoholic drink - a whole drink, not just a sip? **Please don't count drinks labelled low alcohol.**

- Yes [1] — Go to Question 30
- No [2] — Go to Question 43

8

N1448 Aut98 V4

30. How old were you when you had your first proper alcoholic drink?
Write in the box your **age then** in numbers, not words.

I was ▢ years old - Go to Question 31

31. How often do you **usually** have an alcoholic drink?

- Almost every day ▢ 1
- About twice a week ▢ 2
- About once a week ▢ 3
- About once a fortnight ▢ 4 — Go to Question 32
- About once a month ▢ 5
- Only a few times a year ▢ 6
- I never drink alcohol now ▢ 7

32. When you drink alcohol, who are you **usually** with?

- My girlfriend or boyfriend ▢ 1
- Friends of the same sex as me ▢ 2
- Friends of the opposite sex ▢ 3
- A group of friends of both sexes ▢ 4 — Go to Question 33
- My parents (or step-parents) ▢ 5
- My brother, sister, or other relatives ▢ 6
- On my own ▢ 7

33. And when you drink alcohol, where are you **usually**?

- In a pub or bar ▢ 1
- In a club or disco ▢ 2
- At a party with friends ▢ 3 — Go to Question 34
- At my home or someone else's home ▢ 4
- Somewhere else ▢ 5

9

N1448 Apr/98 V4

34. If you buy alcohol, where do you **usually** buy it?

- In a pub or bar ▢ 1
- In a club or disco ▢ 2
- From an off-licence ▢ 3
- From a shop or supermarket ▢ 4 — **Go to Question 35**
- From a friend/relative ▢ 5
- From someone else ▢ 6
- I never buy alcohol ▢ 7

35. When did you **last** have an alcoholic drink?

- Today ▢ 1
- Yesterday ▢ 2 — **Go to Question 35a**
- Some other time during the last week ▢ 3
- 1 week, but less than 2 weeks ago ▢ 4
- 2 weeks, but less than 4 weeks ago ▢ 5 — **Go to Question 43**
- 1 month, but less than 6 months ago ▢ 6
- 6 months ago or more ▢ 7

35a. On which of these days last week did you have an alcoholic drink?
Tick whichever apply

- Sunday ▢ 1
- Monday ▢ 2
- Tuesday ▢ 3
- Wednesday ▢ 4 — **Go to Question 36**
- Thursday ▢ 5
- Friday ▢ 6
- Saturday ▢ 7

10

N1448 Aug/98 V4

38. During the **last 7 days**, how much SHANDY have you drunk?

Have not drunk shandy
in the last 7 days — 1 → Go to Question 39

Less than half a pint — 2

Half a pint or more — 3 → Go to Question 38a

38a. Write in the boxes below the number of pints, half pints, large cans, small cans of SHANDY drunk in the last 7 days.

pints

half pints

large cans

small cans

→ Go to Question 39

39. During the **last 7 days**, how much WINE have you drunk?

Have not drunk wine
in the last 7 days — 1 → Go to Question 40

Less than a glass — 2

One glass or more — 3 → Go to Question 39a

39a. Write in the box below, the number of glasses of WINE drunk in the last 7 days.

— 2 → Go to Question 40

12

N1448 Acc/98 V4

---

36. During the **last 7 days**, how much BEER, LAGER AND CIDER have you drunk? Please don't count drinks labelled low alcohol.

Have not drunk beer, lager or cider
in the last 7 days — 1 → Go to Question 37

Less than half a pint — 2

Half a pint or more — 3 → Go to Question 36a

36a. Write in the boxes below the number of pints, half pints, large cans, small cans, bottles of BEER, LAGER AND CIDER drunk in the last 7 days.

pints

half pints

large cans

small cans

bottles

→ Go to Question 37

37. Do you usually drink normal strength or strong beer? If you usually drink both normal and strong beer, please tick the type you drank most recently.

Normal strength beer — 1 → Go to Question 38

Strong beer — 2

11

N1448 Acc/98 V4

40. During the **last 7 days**, how much MARTINI AND SHERRY have you drunk?

    Have not drunk martini or sherry in the last 7 days   □ 1   **Go to Question 41**

    Less than a glass   □ 2   **Go to Question 41**

    One glass or more   □ 3   **Go to Question 40a**

40a. Write in the box below, the number of glasses of MARTINI OR SHERRY drunk in the last 7 days.

    □   **Go to Question 41**

41. During the **last 7 days**, how much SPIRITS (e.g. whisky, vodka, gin) AND LIQUEURS have you drunk?

    By a glass we mean a single pub measure

    Have not drunk spirits or liqueurs in the last 7 days   □ 1   **Go to Question 42**

    Less than a glass   □ 2   **Go to Question 42**

    One glass or more   □ 3   **Go to Question 41a**

41a. Write in the box below, the number of glasses of SPIRITS (e.g. whisky, vodka, gin) AND LIQUEURS drunk in the last 7 days.

    □   **Go to Question 42**

42. During the **last 7 days**, how much ALCOHOLIC LEMONADE, ALCOHOLIC COLA or OTHER ALCOHOLIC SOFT DRINKS (e.g. Hooch, Two Dogs, Lemonhead) have you drunk?

    Have not drunk alcoholic lemonade, alcoholic cola or other alcoholic soft drinks in the last 7 days   □ 1   **Go to Question 43**

    Less than half a bottle   □ 2   **Go to Question 43**

    One bottle or more   □ 3   **Go to Question 42a**

42a. Write in the boxes below the number of bottles and cans of ALCOHOLIC LEMONADE, ALCOHOLIC COLA and OTHER ALCOHOLIC SOFT DRINKS (e.g. Hooch, Two Dogs, Lemonhead) drunk in the last 7 days.

    □ bottles

    □ cans   **Go to Question 43**

43. Have you ever heard of the following?

Cannabis (Marijuana, Dope, Pot, Blow, Hash, Black, Grass, Draw, Ganja, Spliff, Joints, Smoke, Weed) — 1

Amphetamines (Speed, Uppers, Whizz, Sulphate, Billy, Sulph) — 2

LSD (Acid, Tabs, Trips, Stars, White Lightning) — 3

Ecstasy ('E', Dennis the menace, XTC, X, MDMA) — 4

Semeron (Mop, Bang) — 5

Poppers (Amyl Nitrates, Liquid Gold, TNT, Ram, Rush, Nitrates) — 6

Tranquillisers (Downers, Barbiturates, Blues, Temazies, Jellies, Tranx, Vallies, Benzos, Norries, Moggies, Eggs, Ruggers, Temazapam) — 7

Heroin (Morphine, Smack, Skag, 'H', Brown, Junk) — 8

Magic Mushrooms (Psilocybin, Mushies) — 9

Methadone (Phy, Meth) — 10

Crack (Rock, Sand, Stone, Pebbles) — 11

Cocaine (Coke, Charlie, Snow, Base) — 12

Anabolic Steroids — 13

Any other type of drug — 14

— Go to Question 44

N1448 Att/98 V4

15

---

44. Have you ever been offered any of the following?

Cannabis (Marijuana, Dope, Pot, Blow, Hash, Black, Grass, Draw, Ganja, Spliff, Joints, Smoke, Weed) — 1

Amphetamines (Speed, Uppers, Whizz, Sulphate, Billy, Sulph) — 2

LSD (Acid, Tabs, Trips, Stars, White Lightning) — 3

Ecstasy ('E', Dennis the menace, XTC, X, MDMA) — 4

Semeron (Mop, Bang) — 5

Poppers (Amyl Nitrates, Liquid Gold, TNT, Ram, Rush, Nitrates) — 6

Tranquillisers (Downers, Barbiturates, Blues, Temazies, Jellies, Tranx, Vallies, Benzos, Norries, Moggies, Eggs, Ruggers, Temazapam) — 7 — Go to Question 45

Heroin (Morphine, Smack, Skag, 'H', Brown, Junk) — 8

Magic Mushrooms (Psilocybin, Mushies) — 9

Methadone (Phy, Meth) — 10

Crack (Rock, Sand, Stone, Pebbles) — 11

Cocaine (Coke, Charlie, Snow, Base) — 12

Anabolic Steroids — 13

Glue or Solvents — 14

Any other type of drug — 15

45. Have you ever used or taken any of these? (even if only once)

Yes — 1 — Go to Question 46

No — 2 — Go to Question 48

46. How old were you the first time you used or took any of these? Write in the box your **age then**, in numbers not words.

I was [ ] years old — Go to Question 47

16

N1448 Att/98 V4

48. Please read the following statements about drugs and say if you agree or disagree with each one. *Tick one box for each statement.*

	Agree	Disagree	Don't know
a. Taking drugs is exciting	☐	☐	☐
b. Taking drugs harms your health	☐	☐	☐
c. I don't know enough about the danger of drugs	☐	☐	☐
d. Most young people will try out drugs at some time	☐	☐	☐
e. I wouldn't know what to do if a friend offered me drugs	☐	☐	☐
f. People take drugs to relax	☐	☐	☐
g. I know people my age who take drugs	☐	☐	☐
h. People who take drugs want to escape from reality	☐	☐	☐
i. Drugs are not as harmful as people say they are	☐	☐	☐
j. People who take drugs are stupid	☐	☐	☐

Go to Question 49

N1448 Aug98 V4

---

47. When was the last time you ever used or took any of the following, if ever?
Tick one box only for each drug

	In the last month	In the last year	More than a year ago	Never
Cannabis (Marijuana, Dope, Pot, Blow, Hash, Black, Grass, Draw, Ganja, Spliff, Joints, Smoke, weed)	☐	☐	☐	☐
Amphetamines (Speed, Uppers, Whizz, Sulphate, Billy, Sulph)	☐	☐	☐	☐
LSD (Acid, Tabs, Trips, Stars, White Lightning)	☐	☐	☐	☐
Ecstasy ('E', Dennis the menace, XTC, X, MDMA)	☐	☐	☐	☐
Semeron (Mop, Bang)	☐	☐	☐	☐
Poppers (Amyl Nitrates, Liquid Gold, TNT, Ram, Rush, Nitrates)	☐	☐	☐	☐
Tranquillisers (Downers, Barbiturates, Blues, Temazies, Jellies, Tranx, Vallies, Benzos, Norries, Moggies, Eggs, Ruggers, Temazapam)	☐	☐	☐	☐
Heroin (Morphine, Smack, Skag, 'H', Brown, Junk)	☐	☐	☐	☐
Magic Mushrooms (Psilocybin, Mushies)	☐	☐	☐	☐
Methadone (Phy, Meth)	☐	☐	☐	☐
Crack (Rock, Sand, Stone, Pebbles)	☐	☐	☐	☐
Cocaine (Coke, Charlie, Snow, Base)	☐	☐	☐	☐
Anabolic Steroids	☐	☐	☐	☐
Glue or Solvents	☐	☐	☐	☐
Any other type of drug	☐	☐	☐	☐

Go to Question 48

N1448 Aug98 V4

49. During the last year have you had any lessons, films or discussions in class on the following topics :

	Yes	No	Don't know
How to look after your teeth?	1	2	3
Information about exercise and sports?	1	2	3
Risks of subathing and sunburn?	1	2	3
Healthy eating?	1	2	3
Smoking?	1	2	3
Alcohol?	1	2	3
Sex education/safe sex?	1	2	3
AIDS?	1	2	3
Heroin?	1	2	3
Crack?	1	2	3
Solvent abuse/glue sniffing?	1	2	3
Ecstasy?	1	2	3
Drugs in general?	1	2	3

Go to Question 50

50. Were there any questions you meant to go back and complete? Please check.

If you have finished, please complete the diary next, starting with yesterday and working backwards through the week.

19

N1448 Ao/98 V4